DAVID C. COOK

Discipleship Junction

Talking with God

Sheila Seifert and Beth Naylor

NEXGEN

Building the New Generation of Believers

COOK COMMUNICATIONS MINISTRIES
Colorado Springs, Colorado • Paris, Ontario
KINGSWAY COMMUNICATIONS LTD
Eastbourne, England

NexGen® is an imprint of
Cook Communications Ministries
Colorado Springs, CO 80918
Cook Communications, Paris, Ontario
Kingsway Communications, Eastbourne, England

TALKING WITH GOD
© 2006 by Cook Communications Ministries

Cover Design: BMB Design
Cover Illustration: BMB Design/Ryan Putnam
Interior Design: TrueBlue Design/Sandy Flewelling
Interior Illustrations: Aline Heiser, Anne Kennedy, Chris Sharp

First Printing, 2006
Printed in Canada

1 2 3 4 5 6 7 8 9 10 Printing/Year 11 10 09 08 07 06

ISBN-10: 0-78144-321-0
ISBN-13: 978-0-7814-4321-0

Table of Contents

WELCOME TO DISCIPLESHIP JUNCTION!

Discipleship Junction is an all-new program that harnesses the power of FUN to build young disciples through interaction with Bible truth and with each other.

A complete, multi-age children's ministry program, *Discipleship Junction* is packed full of interactive stories and drama, Scripture memory, and themed snacks and activities that will engage every child! It is guaranteed effective because its principles and methods of instruction are *teacher-tested* and *kid-approved*!

Intensive student-teacher interaction within a learning community that is relational and supportive makes *Discipleship Junction* an ideal program for including children with disabilities. Hands-on learning activities are easily adapted to include all students. For more ideas about inclusion, an excellent resource is *Let All the Children Come to Me* by MaLesa Breeding Ed.D., Dana Hood, Ph.D., and Jerry Whitworth, Ed.D. (Colorado Springs: Cook Communications Ministries, 2006).

Putting the Pieces Together

Get Set. We know you're busy, so we provide a list of materials and what you'll need to prepare for your lesson. You'll also need a photocopy machine and some basic classroom supplies: paper, pencils, markers, butcher paper, scissors, glue, and index cards. When you see this icon allow a little extra prep time.

Kids love to dress up! Many of our Bible lessons use costume props from the *Bible time dress-up box*. This can be as simple as a box of items you gather from around the house or purchase inexpensively from a secondhand store. It should

include: old sheet with neck hole (angel), fake beard, swords, head cloths and brow bands, bathrobes, fancy "princess" dress, crown, decorative chains and belts for temple priests, shepherd's crook or stick, wolf ears, wigs.

Tickets Please! *(10 minutes)* Each week begins with an activity option to involve children while others are being dropped off by parents.

- The *Welcome Time Activity* will excite children's interest and help them connect with the Bible Truth for the week.

- *Sweet treats.* Children are rewarded for attendance with a treat. God is pleased when children come and talk to Him. Whenever they do, He rewards them with His presence. The treats remind us of that reward. Just fill a large jar with individually wrapped treats such as small candies, fruit snacks, etc. Avoid foods typically associated with allergies, such as nuts. If you have students who are diabetic, remember to include sugar-free candies.

All Aboard for Bible Truth! *(20 minutes).* Whole group, interactive Bible lessons invite students ages 6–11 to participate in the entire lesson. Whether it's role-playing a hailstorm or squeezing through an obstacle course, kids will be engaged in exciting, hands-on lessons.

- Pre- and post-lesson discussion times encourage children to talk about their own life experiences and tie their knowledge to the week's Bible Truth.

- *Use the Clues!* Practice is an important part of learning, and helps us move information from short-term to long-term memory. Every week one significant object from the lesson is added to the *Use the Clues!* bag. In the weeks that follow, students are repeatedly challenged to remember the Bible Truths connected with the objects. These "memory hooks" help Bible Truth stick with kids for a long time to come.

Bible Memory Waypoint *(5 minutes)*. Toe tappin' and finger snappin' . . . there's nothing like the power of fun to motivate children. Movement, rhythm, and roleplay make it easy for kids to hide God's Word in their hearts (Psalm 119:11).

Prayer Station *(15 minutes)*. Small-group prayer time for children. Wow! What an idea! Children break into small groups of three to five with an adult helper—we call them StationMasters. Using reproducible instruction cards, adults guide children to explore and practice new prayer skills. Together they'll share concerns, praise God, and practice the four activities of prayer: *praise, ask, confess, give thanks.*

(Optional) ***Snack Stop and Activities*** *(10 minutes)*. Tied to the theme of the lesson, you have options for snacks and activities in which lesson truths are practiced and shared. Look for the throttle icon which shows the level of mess, energy, or noise required for the activity!

On the Fast Track! Reproducible take-home pages invite families to interact in and through fun activities and Bible memory.

Are you looking for an additional way to motivate young learners? *Discipleship Junction* includes an optional incentive program which rewards students for completing take-home pages. Children return a signed *Fast Track!* ticket and choose a prize from the treasure box. If you have a new student, you might welcome that child with the choice of a treasure too! Simply cover and decorate a large shoebox. Fill with inexpensive items such as you might find at a party store.

HOW TO GET STARTED

1. ***Begin by recruiting StationMasters***—adult helpers who will guide children through the process of praying in small groups. Don't have enough adult volunteers? How about recruiting middle- or high-schoolers to shepherd a group? Also consider enlisting a few faithful prayer partners who will commit to praying for your class weekly.

   Plan to have a brief training session with your volunteers in which you'll explain how to usethe *imPACT* model of prayer . Each week you'll give the StationMasters a reproducible instruction card with the day's prayer theme and prayer suggestions to use with children in a small group.

2. ***Set up your room.*** You'll need a big area for your large-group Bible teaching time. You'll also need to identify spaces for each of your small prayer groups. Don't forget that moving chairs and tables, or moving groups to a hallway is always an option. And children are willing helpers!

3. ***Photocopy reproducible letters*** (see Resources) for parents and children's ministry helpers. Mail these two or three weeks before you begin your children's ministry program.

4. ***Photocopy On the Fast Track!*** pages for each child, and ***StationMaster Cards*** for each adult helper. If you choose, make copies of the reproducibles for all the lessons ahead of time. This can save a last-minute scramble when time is tight!

5. **Gather and prepare your materials**, set out your snacks, and you are ready to roll. So . . . **FULL SPEED AHEAD! ALL ABOARD FOR DISCIPLESHIP JUNCTION!**

LESSON ONE: The Day the Sun Stood Still

Memory Verse:

The LORD is my strength and my shield; my heart trusts in him and I am helped. My heart leaps for joy and I will give thanks to him in song (Psalm 28:7). *Note: Early elementary verse in **bold** type.*

Bible Basis:
Joshua 10

Bible Truth:
We pray because we trust God and depend on Him.

Why do we pray?

You Will Need:

- [ ] Bible time dress-up box
- [ ] craft pompoms – a handful
- [ ] yellow ball
- [ ] butcher paper
- [ ] 1 poster board
- [ ] treat jar
- [ ] *Use the Clues!* bag
- [ ] *On the Fast Track! #1* take-home paper
- [ ] *StationMaster Card #1*
- [ ] (Optional) treasure box
- [ ] (Optional) Snack: small paper cups or coffee filters, popcorn
- [ ] (Optional) Activity: large plastic tablecloth, unpopped popcorn kernels, popcorn popper

 When you see this icon, it means preparation will take more than five minutes.

 GET SET!
(Lesson Preparation)

- ■ 🌐 Print today's Bible memory verse on a poster board:
  The LORD is my strength and my shield; my heart trusts in him, and I am helped. My heart leaps for joy and I will give thanks to him in song (Psalm 28:7).
  Hang the poster board on the wall at the front of the classroom.
- ■ Print "We depend on God" on the ball with black marker.
- ■ Make a copy of *On the Fast Track #1* take-home paper for each child.
- ■ Make a copy of *StationMaster Card #1* for each helper.
- ■ Set out the treat jar, *Use the Clues!* bag, and (optional) treasure box.
- ■ Set up snack or outside play activities if you include these items in your children's ministry.
- ■ Tape a 10-foot length of butcher paper to a flat wall at children's eye level; set boxes of markers or crayons on the floor in front of it.

TICKETS PLEASE!
(Welcome and Bible Connection)

- ■ *Objective: To excite children's interest and connect their own life experiences with the Bible Truth, children will make a mural and talk about depending on God.*

Welcome Time Activity: Make-a-Mural

■ *Materials:* *Butcher paper, markers or crayons, tape*
As children arrive, direct them to the wall where you have taped the butcher paper. Have your adult or teen helpers (StationMasters) invite children to work together to draw a picture of some of the things for which they depend on God (for help in trouble, for healing when sick, for parents, for food, for His presence).

When everyone has arrived, call children to the lesson area and welcome them. Offer them a treat from the treat jar. Say: **God likes it when children come and talk to Him. Whenever they do, He rewards them with His presence. The treats remind us of that reward.** Children may finish their treat now, or set it aside to take home later.

Sharing Time and Bible Connection

Introduce today's lesson by discussing these questions with your students in the large group. As you talk, give every child the opportunity to say something.

■ **What kinds of things are very hard or maybe even scary for you to do?**
■ **How do you feel when a friend wants to be with you and help you with those things?** (thankful, happy)
■ **When you are afraid, sad, or have something hard to do, who do you depend on for help? Why?** (parents, friends)

After this sharing time, help your students connect their discussion to the Bible story they are about to hear from Joshua 10:
God wants to be your best friend. He is always there to listen to us and talk with us. But how can we talk to God? We can't even see Him! Pause to let children respond. **Yes, prayer is talking to God. <u>We pray because we trust God and depend on Him.</u> In today's Bible story, a man named Joshua was in great danger. He needed help *fast*! Who do you think he talked to? Right! He talked to God! Let's learn more about it.**

ALL ABOARD FOR BIBLE TRUTH!   Joshua 10
(Bible Discover and Learn Time)

■ *Objective:* *Children will study Joshua 10 and hear that Joshua prayed because he depended on God.*
■ *Materials:* *Bible time dress-up box, yellow ball with "We depend on God" printed on it*

I'm going to need five of you to help me tell this story. Give each person a prop and

ask them to stand across the front of the room where everyone can see them. Then say:

(Name) **wearing the beard is Joshua. When I point to Joshua, everyone should cheer, "Hooray!" Joshua, you should flex your muscles like a hero. Try that.**

(Name) **wearing the crown represents the five kings and their armies. When I point to the king, everyone should to say, "Boo!" King, you should make a mean face and shake your fist at us. Show us.** Have the children practice cheering and booing as you point to Joshua and the king. Have an older helper wear the crown. It may be too hard for younger children to have "boos" directed at them.

(Name) **holding the sword will swish his/her sword TWICE for the battle. Only twice. When I point to the battle, everyone else should punch the air twice and say, "Biff! Pow!" Try it.** Caution against punching or sword fighting other students.

(Name holding the pompoms), **show us what you're holding. What does this look like? Those are hailstones! When I point to the hailstones, you should all slap your lap with your hands to make the hail sound. Practice that. Hail, listen carefully for your part in the story. You'll know what to do!**

(Name) **holding the yellow ball is the sun. When I point to the sun you should all say, "Ooooo." Sun, you should walk in very slow circles around this group of story helpers. Don't stop until you hear your part in the story. Listen very carefully! Begin your orbit now.**

Let the children practice saying "Hooray!," "Boo," "Biff! Pow!," as you point to each story helper. **Very good! Now let's begin our story. Today's Bible story about Joshua** (point to Joshua and prompt children to say "Hooray!") **comes from the Old Testament.**

After Moses, the leader of Israel, died, God chose a new leader—Joshua (point to Joshua). **Joshua was a faithful man who listened to God and obeyed Him. One day, God told Joshua to lead the people of Israel across the river to the land He had promised to give them. It was a wonderful land, full of good things. But the land was ruled by five kings** (point to the king and prompt children to say "Boo") **with vast armies who did not love God or worship Him. The** *bad news* **was that before Israel could move into the land, God said they would have to fight a battle with the kings** (point to the battle). **The** *good news* **was that God said He would help them win.**

The kings were afraid! "We cannot fight (point to Joshua) **Joshua alone," they said. "He is too strong." So the five kings** (point to the king) **joined together and sent their armies of soldiers against Joshua in battle.**

Imagine . . . five armies! But God told Joshua, "Do not be afraid of the five kings or their armies. Not one of them will be able to beat you in battle (point to battle). Joshua depended on God **to help him win.**

All night Joshua and his army marched. The next morning, he came upon the five kings by surprise. The Lord made the five armies confused and afraid. What do you think those (point to the king) **five armies did?** Pause for children to respond. **Yes, they ran away!**

Joshua (point to Joshua) **and the army of Israel chased them down the road. As they ran, the Lord threw large hailstones** (point to hailstones) **down on them from the sky.** Pause for hail to fall on king. **The Lord was fighting for Israel.**

But the battle (point to battle) **was not over yet! Joshua needed more time. So he prayed, "Lord, please make the sun** (point to the sun) **stand still until we finish fighting with our enemies." And do you know what happened?** Pause for children to respond. **The** (point to the sun) **sun . . . stood . . . STILL.** Wait for the sun to stop walking. **It stopped in the middle of the sky for a whole day while Israel battled** (point to battle). **The sun** (point to the sun) **stood still until Israel had won. It was a miracle from God! There has never been a day like it before or since.** Thank the volunteers for their help and have them sit down again.

> ***Story Option:*** *In place of the dress-ups, you may elect to have volunteers hold up large picture posters of Joshua, the kings, the battle, the hail, and the sun. Note that you would need to draw these large pictures ahead of time. Stick figures are fine.*

Use the Clues!
(Bible Review)

Okay, let's see what you remember.

■ **What did God tell Joshua to do?** (move into the promised land, fight the people who lived there)

■ **How do you think Joshua felt when he saw the five armies against him?** (afraid, nervous)

■ **How did Joshua show he trusted God?** (Joshua prayed and asked God for help)

■ **What did Joshua ask God to do?** (He asked God to make the sun stand still so he could finish the battle)

■ **How can we show that we trust God and need Him for everything?** (We can talk to Him about things that trouble us, too)

■ **Do we need God to help us fight armies?** (No, of course not) **What do we depend on God for?**

When Joshua needed help, he talked to God. Joshua prayed and asked God for an amazing long day. God wants us to talk to Him too, because it shows that we trust Him and need Him for everything. Take the ball out of the bag and say: **Here's a yellow ball that reminds us of the sun in our Bible story today. The words on it say, "We depend on God." I am going to toss it to someone and when you catch it, you should say, "We depend on God." Then I want you to gently toss it to someone else who will say, "We depend on God."** Once everyone has had a chance to catch the ball, put it in the *Use the Clues!* bag. Say: **The yellow ball will remind us how Joshua asked God to stop the sun. Joshua needed God for everything. We depend on God too.**

Show the *Use the Clues!* bag. **Every week after our story we will put an object in the bag to help us remember what we have learned that week.** Put the ball in the bag.

BIBLE MEMORY WAYPOINT!
(Scripture Memory)

Psalm 28:7

■ **Objective:** *Children will hide God's Word in their hearts for guidance, protection, and encouragement.*

Read this week's memory verse from the poster. Point to each word as you read it:

The LORD is my strength and my shield; my heart trusts in him, and I am helped. My heart leaps for joy and I will give thanks to him in song (Psalm 28:7).

To help children memorize the Bible verse, have them act it out with you:

The LORD *(bow down to a king)*
is my strength *(show your muscles)*
and my shield; *(place both hands in front of you to form a shield)*
my heart trusts in him, *(pat your hand on your chest to sound like a heartbeat)*
and I am helped. *(grasp one hand with the other and shake it)*
My heart leaps for joy *(jump into the air)*
and I will give thanks *(kiss your fingers and fling the kiss to heaven)*
to him in song. *(sing "la-la-la")*
(Psalm 28:7)

Act out the memory verse with them several times so they become familiar with it. If time allows, have the group turn around and say the verse again *without* looking at the poster. *Be sure to include the Bible reference too!*

PRAYER STATION

■ **Objective:** *Children will explore and practice prayer for themselves in small groups.*
■ **Materials:** *Copies of* StationMaster Card #1 *for each adult or teen helper*

Break the large group into smaller groups of three to five children. Assign a teen or adult helper to each small group and give each helper a copy of *StationMaster Card #1* (see Resources) with ideas for group discussion and prayer.

SNACK STOP: HEAVENLY HAILSTONES (Optional)

If you plan to provide a snack, this is an ideal time to serve it.

■ *Materials: a small paper cup or coffee filter for each child, popped popcorn*

Fill paper cups with popcorn. As children snack, talk with them about the hailstorm in today's Bible story.

Note: Always be aware of children with food allergies and have another option on hand if necessary.

 ## APPLICATION

■ *Objective: Children will have opportunities to show how the lesson works in their own lives through activities and take-home papers.*

Some children's ministries may allow children to play outside at this point. If yours does not, choose one of the following activities.

 ### Freeze

Today we learned that Joshua depended on God to make the sun stand still. Tell the children that they are like the sun, which is constantly moving. They should walk around the room until you say "Freeze!"

When you say "Freeze!" everyone should stand still. If someone moves, touch that child on the shoulder and he can help you find others who are moving the next time you say "Freeze!" Continue playing until only one person is left. You can proclaim that person the winner and then start the game over.

 ### Hailstorm!

■ *Materials: plastic tablecloth, popcorn popper, unpopped kernels*

Cover the floor with a plastic tablecloth and sit the children on the floor around the perimeter. Set a popcorn popper in the middle of the tablecloth on something firm like a board. Pop some popcorn kernels but leave the lid off the popper. As the popcorn flies in the air, let children eat any kernels that fall in front of them. Caution them to remain seated and wait until kernels are cool.

 ### ON THE FAST TRACK! *(Take-Home Papers)*

(Optional) Introduce the treasure box by asking: **Who would like to choose a prize from the treasure box?** Anticipate excited responses. **Today I'm going to give every child an *On the Fast Track!* paper to take home. There are activities to do and a Bible verse to memorize on each sheet. To earn a prize, you must complete all the activities at home this week and learn your verse. When you are finished, ask your parents or another adult to sign the ticket on the front and bring it with you next week when you come. If you do, you'll get to choose a prize from the treasure box!**

Distribute the take-home papers just before children leave.

Memory Verse:

Blessed is the man . . . [whose] delight is in the law of the LORD, and on his law he meditates day and night (Psalm 1:1-2).

Bible Basis:

1 Samuel 16 and Psalm 29

Why do we pray?

Bible Truth:

We pray because God is delighted to talk with us.

You Will Need:

- [ ] 1 poster board
- [ ] any and all puppets available or paper bags
- [ ] 1 small stuffed lamb
- [ ] white adhesive labels marked with 11 different colors
- [ ] each verse of Psalm 29 printed out on a separate piece of paper
- [ ] treat jar
- [ ] *Use the Clues!* bag and previous item
- [ ] *On the Fast Track! #2* take-home paper
- [ ] *StationMaster Card #2*
- [ ] *(Optional)* treasure box
- [ ] *(Optional)* Snack: round sugar cookies or bread slices; white frosting or whipped cream cheese; choice of raisins, dried cranberries, chocolate chips, or M&Ms; plastic knives
- [ ] *(Optional)* Activity: balloons

When you see this icon, it means preparation will take more than five minutes.

GET SET!
(Lesson Preparation)

- ■ ⏱ Print today's Bible memory verse on a poster board:

  Blessed is the man whose delight is in the law of the LORD, and on his law he meditates day and night (Psalm 1:1-2).

  Hang the poster board on the wall at the front of the classroom.

- ■ Print "Prayer makes God happy" on an index card and tape it to the stuffed lamb.

- ■ ⏱ Color adhesive labels with 11 different colors. Make sure you have one label for each child in your class.

- ■ ⏱ Type each verse of Psalm 29 on a separate piece of paper, including the reference at the bottom (e.g. Psalm 29:1, Psalm 29:2, etc.).

- ■ Make a copy of *On the Fast Track #2* take-home paper for each child.

- ■ Make a copy of *StationMaster Card #2* for each helper.

- ■ Set out the treat jar, *Use the Clues!* bag, and *(optional)* treasure box.

- ■ Set up snack or outside play activities if you include these items in your children's ministry.

TICKETS PLEASE!
(Welcome and Bible Connection)

■ **Objective:** *To excite children's interest and connect their own experiences with the Bible Truth, children will do puppet play and talk about things that make them happy.*

Welcome Time Activity: Puppet Play

■ **Materials:** *any and all puppets available OR paper bags and markers for children to create a bag puppet*

As children arrive, let them choose a puppet to play with. Have them talk to the puppet or interact with another child's puppet. Encourage them to talk about things that make them happy. Alternately, children can create a simple puppet by drawing a face, hair, and clothes on a lunch-size paper bag.

When everyone has arrived, go around the room and stick an adhesive label marked with color to each child's upper body. Ask them to leave the label in place for an activity later. Welcome the children and offer them a treat from the treat jar. Say: **Be happy about eating this candy because God is happy when you come to learn about Him and talk to Him.** Children may finish their treat now, or set it aside to take home later.

(Optional) If children hand you a *Fast Track!* ticket, they may pick a prize from the treasure box.

Sharing Time and Bible Connection

Introduce today's lesson by discussing these questions with your students in the large group. As you talk, give every child the opportunity to respond.

■ **How do you feel when a friend calls you or sends you a message?** (happy, glad)
■ **Why do you feel that way when you hear from a good friend?** (it shows they care about you)
■ **When someone you like doesn't talk to you, how do you feel?** (sad, hurt, lonely)

After discussion time, help your students connect their ideas to the Bible story they're about to hear from 1 Samuel 16 and Psalm 29:

God feels happy when we talk to Him. When we pray to Him, He is so pleased! He loves to hear from us, any time and anywhere. When we don't pray, God misses hearing from us. That's another reason we pray—because <u>God is delighted to talk with us.</u> In today's Bible story, a shepherd had lots of time to talk to God. He even wrote songs and sang them to God. How do you think God felt about that? (delighted, pleased, loved) **Let's find out more.**

ALL ABOARD FOR BIBLE TRUTH!   1 Samuel 16 and Psalm 29
(Bible Discover and Learn Time)

- ■ *Objective:* Children will study 1 Samuel 16 and Psalm 29 and hear that David prayed because God delights in hearing from His people.
- ■ *Materials:* white adhesive labels marked with 11 different colors, enough for every child to have one, 1 small stuffed lamb with the "Prayer makes God happy" card taped to it

Have you heard of a shepherd named David? Let children answer. **He was going to be the king of Israel. But first, God had other work for him—being a shepherd. What does a shepherd do?** Wait for response. **He takes care of sheep and protects them from wild animals. He herds them to where they can find food and water.**

You may not know this, but sheep don't move too fast, especially when they're eating. Show me how you think sheep would move. Wait while children demonstrate. Affirm their actions. **While the sheep are grazing and eating grass, what do you think the shepherd does?** Wait for children to answer.

That's right. He sits and watches them for hours and hours and hours. Show me by making a face how you would feel about that job. Because David had so much time watching the sheep eat, he talked to God a lot. He listened to God too. He liked to sing, so he made up songs and sang them to God. They were like musical prayers.

<u>**The Bible says God was delighted whenever David talked to Him.**</u> **God loved the time that David spent with Him so much that He called David a man after His own heart. That means David knew God very well because he talked to God so often. The musical prayers David wrote are called psalms. Have you heard of those before?** Let children respond. **We're going to play a game using one of David's psalms to God.**

Use the color-coded adhesive labels to divide the children into groups. The reds will be one group, the blues another group, etc. Adjust groups if there are too many young children in one group. Make sure that there is a strong reader in each group. Hand each group a sheet of paper printed with one verse from Psalm 29.

Each group will have one reader. The rest of the group will become statues. Tell children: **Read the verse on your sheet of paper and then arrange yourselves so that your statue demonstrates that verse.** Give the students four to five minutes to decide how their human statue will look. Helpers should go from group to group helping children refine their ideas and understand their Bible verse.

When groups are ready, have the group with verse one begin the psalm. While the group forms a statue, their reader should read the verse. As the rest of the children clap for the group, the group with the next verse should come forward. They can then form their statue and read their verse. Continue until all eleven verses are completed.

After hearing Psalm 29, how do you think David felt about God? Pass around the stuffed lamb with the card, "Prayer makes God happy." Each child should repeat this sentence before passing it on to the next child. When every child has touched the lamb and said the words, place the lamb in the *Use the Clues!* bag.

The lamb is our reminder of how David was a shepherd. David made God happy by talking to Him. We also make God happy whenever we talk to Him.

Collect all adhesive labels and have children return to the lesson area. Return these to the children at the end of your lesson time.

Use the Clues!
(Bible Review)

Bring out the *Use the Clues!* bag. **Okay, let's see what you remember.** Pull the yellow ball out of bag. **Think back to our Bible story from last week. What does this clue remind us of?** Have children raise their hands. Call on volunteers to name the story. **Yes, our Bible lesson was about Joshua and the day the sun stood still. What did we learn about prayer last week?** (we depend on God)

- **Did you depend on God this week by talking to Him about a problem?** (allow responses)
- **In today's lesson, why did David have so much time?** (shepherd, watched sheep while they ate)
- **What was the best way David used his time?** (talked to God, made up musical prayers)

- **If you follow David's example of talking often to God, how will God feel?** (delighted, happy, pleased to talk with you).
- **Why should you talk to God and listen to Him?** (He's our Lord, a friend, we love Him, we need Him, it delights Him)

David could have used his free time to carve wood or to daydream. He probably did those things too, but he gave God the best of his free time. And because he did, God blessed him and was so happy to have all that time with David. God wants to have time with you, too. **When you pray, you make God happy!** He is so ready to hear what's on your mind every day.

Today's reminder in the *Use the Clues!* bag is (long dramatic pause, then pull out the lamb with the words "Prayer makes God happy"). **This lamb reminds us that David, the shepherd, talked to God often and that delighted God. God is just as delighted when you talk to Him.** Put the lamb and ball back in the bag.

BIBLE MEMORY WAYPOINT!
(Scripture Memory)   Psalm 1:1-2

- ***Objective:*** *Children will hide God's Word in their hearts for guidance, protection, and encouragement.*

Read this week's memory verse from the poster. Point to each word as you read it:

Blessed is the man whose delight is in the law of the Lord, and on his law he meditates day and night (Psalm 1:1-2).

To help children memorize the Bible verse, have them say it with you using different voices:

Blessed is the man (*start "blessed" on a low note and raise your voice higher with each word*)
whose delight is in the law of the Lord, (*clap as you say each syllable*)
and on his law (*start with a low voice and get higher with each word*)
he meditates day and night. (*clap as you say each syllable*)
Psalm 1:1-2

Repeat the memory verse with the different voices a few more times so children become familiar with it.

 ## PRAYER STATION

- ■ *Objective:* Children will explore and practice prayer for themselves.
- ■ *Materials:* copies of StationMaster Card #2 for each adult or teen helper

Break into small groups of three to five children. Assign a teen or adult helper to each small group and give each helper a copy of *StationMaster Card #2* (see Resources Section) with ideas for group discussion and prayer.

 ## SNACK STOP: DELIGHTED SMILES (Optional)

If you plan to provide a snack, this is an ideal time to serve it.

- ■ *Materials: round sugar cookies* or *bread slices cut into circles with cookie cutter or wide drinking cup; white frosting or whipped cream cheese; choice of raisins; dried cranberries, chocolate chips or round chocolate candies; plastic knives*

Children can take turns spreading a thin layer of frosting or cream cheese on their cookie or bread circle. Then make a smiley face with the dried fruit or candy pieces. Discuss what kinds of things children can tell God, reinforcing the truth that prayer makes Him happy.
Note: Always be aware of children with food allergies and have another option on hand if necessary.

APPLICATION

■ **Objective:** *Children will have opportunities to show how the lesson works in their own lives through activities and take-home papers.*

Some children's ministries may allow children to play outside at this point. If yours does not, choose one of the following activities.

 Lamb Tag

David watched a flock of sheep. Have all the children get down on their hands and knees like lambs except for one who is the shepherd. The lambs may go in any direction. The shepherd must try to get the lambs to reach the other side of the room. The lambs must obey the shepherd. Once a lamb successfully reaches the other side of the room, s/he becomes a shepherd and helps to herd the other sheep. The last lamb to reach the other side of the room becomes the shepherd and the game starts over.

 Sheep-herding Practice

Blow up enough balloons for each child to have one, with a few extras in case of popping. Make a "sheep pen" by grouping some chairs or other objects in a corner of the room. The goal is to herd the sheep (balloons) into the sheep pen by batting the balloon into the enclosure. Children should try to bat only their balloon, though happy chaos may follow. When all the sheep are safely in the pen, shepherds can congratulate each other for a job well done, then play again.

 ON THE FAST TRACK! *(Take-Home Papers)*

(Optional) Treasure box: **Who would like to choose a prize from the treasure box?** Remind children about the *On the Fast Track!* take-home papers. **Today I'm going to give every child an *On the Fast Track!* paper to take home. You can do activities and memorize the Bible verse. To earn a prize, you need to finish all the activities at home this week and learn your verse. When you're finished, ask your parents or another adult to sign the *Fast Track!* ticket. Bring it with you next week. Then you'll get to choose a prize from the treasure box!**
Distribute the take-home papers just before children leave.

LESSON THREE: Queen Esther Saves the Jews

Memory Verse:

For we are God's workmanship, created in Christ Jesus to do good works, which God prepared in advance for us to do (Ephesians 2:10).

*Note: Early elementary verse in **bold** type.*

Bible Basis:

Book of Esther

Bible Truth:

We pray because God allows us to be involved in His work.

You Will Need:

- [ ] Bible time dress-up box
- [ ] flower seeds
- [ ] 1 poster board
- [ ] 1 flowerpot with dirt
- [ ] 1 photograph of your family
- [ ] 1 watering can
- [ ] small trowel or craft stick
- [ ] an adult who has had prayer change his/her family
- [ ] treat jar
- [ ] *Use the Clues!* bag and previous objects
- [ ] *On the Fast Track! #3* take-home paper
- [ ] *StationMaster Card #3*
- [ ] *(Optional)* treasure box
- [ ] *(Optional)* Snack: flour tortillas, kitchen scissors or knife, spreadable jam or jelly, napkins
- [ ] *(Optional)* Activity: large whiteboard or several sheets of poster board, markers

 When you see this icon, it means preparation will take more than five minutes.

GET SET!
(Lesson Preparation)

- Print today's Bible memory verse on a poster board: **For we are God's workmanship, created in Christ Jesus to do good works, which God prepared in advance for us to do (Ephesians 2:10).** Hang the poster board on the wall at the front of the classroom.
- Print "God lets me be part of His plan" on an index card and tape it to the family photograph.
- Make a copy of *On the Fast Track #3* take-home paper for each child.
- Make a copy of *StationMaster Card #3* for each helper.
- Set out the treat jar, *Use the Clues!* bag, and *(optional)* treasure box.
- Set up snack or outside play activities if you include these items in your children's ministry.

TICKETS PLEASE!
(Welcome and Bible Connection)

- ***Objective:*** *To excite children's interest and connect their own experiences with the Bible Truth, children will play a game, "The King/Queen Says."*

Welcome Time Activity: The King/Queen Says

As children arrive, start them playing "The King/Queen Says." Adapt "Simon Says" by substituting "The King says . . ." or "The Queen says . . ." Children should take turns commanding other players what actions to make. If they say "The King/Queen Says" first, players should do the action. If they don't say those words, players shouldn't do the action. When players are "caught," they must sit out until the King or Queen changes. Actions can be anything active, such as jumping, clapping, arm swinging, tummy rubbing, etc. Let a King or Queen give five or six commands, then choose another child to take the lead.

When everyone has arrived, welcome the children and offer them a treat from the treat jar. **When you take a treat today, you're letting God know you want to be part of His plan.** Children may finish their treat now, or set it aside to take home later.

(Optional) If children returned a signed *Fast Track!* ticket, they may choose a prize from the treasure box also.

Sharing Time and Bible Connection

■ *Materials: 1 flowerpot with dirt, trowel or craft stick, flower seeds, 1 watering can*

Use this object lesson to introduce today's lesson on prayer. Choose a volunteer and ask: **Would you help me plant flowers?** Act like you're going to let the child plant the seeds, but do all the work yourself. When the task is finished, say: **Wasn't that fun?** As the child sits down, ask the group, **Do you think** (child's name) **liked planting flowers?** Allow children to answer or protest. **How would** (child) **have felt if I let him help?** Allow responses.

■ **Tell us about a time when a parent or other adult asked you to help them do a job.**
■ **How did you feel to be involved in their work?**
■ **Did you ever think that God might want you to be part of His work too?**

After sharing time, help your students connect their discussion to the Bible story from Esther they are about to hear:

God can do everything by Himself. But <u>He allows us to be involved in working out some of His plans.</u> Can you imagine that? The God who created everything <u>lets us be part of His work</u> on Earth. He created us to want to help. Isn't that cool? Let's find out about someone God used in His plan in the Old Testament.

ALL ABOARD FOR BIBLE TRUTH!   Esther
(Bible Discover and Learn Time)

- ■ *Objective:* Children will study Esther and hear that Esther prayed because God wanted to use her in His plan to save the Jews.
- ■ *Materials:* Bible time dress-up box, Use the Clues! bag and previous items, your family photograph

Ask three children to help tell the story. Choose one girl and two boys if possible. Have the girl find a fancy dress from the dress-up box. One boy will be Haman and wear a fancy shirt. The other boy is Mordecai and should wear a robe. Tell the three children that when you point to them, they'll repeat the last line you say.

One whole book of the Bible is about a woman who was <u>allowed to help God</u> in a huge way.

This is Queen Esther. Point to the girl with the dress. **Queen Esther's family was in big trouble.**

This is Haman. Point to the boy in fancy shirt. **Haman is an evil man who is very powerful. He made a rule to kill all the Jews within one year. Haman laughed and said, "I want them all dead!"** Have child laugh and repeat the last line.

This is Mordecai. Point to the boy in the robe. **Mordecai is Queen Esther's uncle. He didn't like Haman's law. It meant his people would all die. So he stood at the king's gate and cried loudly.** Have child cry loudly.

When Queen Esther saw her uncle Mordecai crying, she asked him, "Why are you crying?" Point to Esther and have her repeat the last line.

Mordecai stopped crying and said, "Haman wants to kill our whole family!" Have child repeat the line.

You see, Queen Esther was a Jew. All her family and friends—almost everyone she knew—were Jews. Hearing this news was awful. She asked Mordecai, "What can I do about it?" Have child repeat the line.

Speak strongly. **Mordecai said, "You have to tell the king."** Have child repeat the line.

Queen Esther shook her head. That wouldn't work! She said, "If I go to the king without being invited, I could be killed." Have child repeat the line.

Mordecai knew that Queen Esther was a Jew, and her life was in danger too. But he believed that God could save the Jewish people in any way He wanted. Mordecai told Esther, "Maybe God made you the queen so you could help your family." Have child repeat the line.

Esther knew that Mordecai was right. But she couldn't do this alone. Going to the king without an invitation was very serious. So she told Mordecai, "Tell everyone to fast and pray for me." Have child repeat the line. **What does it mean to fast?** (go without food for a time)

So Mordecai asked their whole family and all their friends to fast and pray for three days for Esther. Mordecai prayed too. "Please help Esther do what you want her to do." Have child repeat the line.

Esther prayed for three days too. Then it was time to go talk to the king. **How do you think she felt?** Let children share. **Instead of killing her, the king listened to her. The king was angry when he heard about Haman's evil plan, and he ordered that Haman and his family be killed instead of the Jewish people. Then he wrote a new law that saved the Jews!** Enthusiastically say: **Esther and Mordecai cheered, "Praise God! He saved our people! God saved us!"** Esther and Mordecai repeat the line.

God could have saved the Jews without Queen Esther and Mordecai. But <u>He let them be a part of the plan. God wanted them to be part of His work.</u>

Thank the volunteers, put away their dress-up clothes, and have them sit down.

Use the Clues!
(Bible Review)

Okay, let's see what else you remember about prayer.
Bring out the *Use the Clues!* bag. Pull the yellow ball out of bag. **Think back to our Bible story from the first week. What does this clue remind us about prayer?** Call on volunteers to name the story and the Bible Truth. (Refer to page 84 for a list of the clues, stories, and prayer truths they represent.) Pull the stuffed lamb out of the bag. **Here is the clue from last week. What does this clue remind us about prayer?**

- **In today's story, what was Queen Esther's problem?** (evil Haman made a law to kill her people, the Jews)
- **What was God's plan?** (to save the Jews)
- **How did Esther become part of God's plan?** (by praying and asking God what He wanted her to do)
- **How can you be involved with the plan God wants to do?** (pray and tell Him we want to be involved, be ready to do what God says)
- Hold up the photograph with the card "God lets me be part of His plan." **This picture of my family is a reminder that <u>God wants us to be part of His plan.</u> We don't know what God's plans are. But when we tell God we want to work with Him, He'll use us when He wants to, like He did with Esther.** Pass the photo around so each child can read the card out loud and pass it on. Then put it in the *Use the Clues!* bag.

BIBLE MEMORY WAYPOINT!
(Scripture Memory)   Ephesians 2:10

- ***Objective:*** *Children will hide God's Word in their hearts for guidance, protection, and encouragement.*

Read this week's memory verse from the poster, pausing at the end of each phrase:
For we are God's workmanship,// created in Christ Jesus// to do good works, which God prepared in advance for us to do (Ephesians 2:10).

To memorize this week's Bible verse, have children sit in chairs set in a circle. You should say the first phrase of the verse, then children will stand up, repeat the phrase, and scoot to the next chair. Once everyone is seated, say the next phrase and children will stand, repeat, and move. Continue through the verse and reference. Do it again, going in the opposite direction. Then try it with kids walking around the circle, saying the verse, then sitting down when done.

PRAYER STATION

- **Objective:** *Children will explore and practice prayer for themselves.*
- **Materials:** *Copies of* StationMaster Card #3 *for each helper*

Break into groups of three to five children. Assign a teen or adult helper to each small group and give each helper a copy of *StationMaster Card #3* (see Resources) with topics for group discussion and prayer.

SNACK STOP: ROYAL ROLL-UPS (Optional)

If you plan to provide a snack, this is an ideal time to serve it.

- **Materials:** *flour tortillas, kitchen scissors or knife, spreadable jam or jelly, napkins*

Cut tortillas in half. Spread a thin smear of jam or jelly, then let children roll them up. As they eat, chat about what might have happened if Esther hadn't prayed and been willing to be part of God's plan to save the Jews.

   Note: Always be aware of children with food allergies and have another option on hand if necessary.

APPLICATION

- **Objective:** *Children will have opportunities to show how the lesson works in their own lives through activities and take-home papers.*

Some children's ministries may allow children to play outside at this point. If yours does not, choose one of the following activities.

Draw-a-Queen Relay

Use a large whiteboard or several sheets of poster board for this game. Divide children into several teams and line them up about 10 feet away from the drawing boards. Give the first person in each line a marker. Write a list of the items to be drawn: body, head, crown, pretty clothes, royal robe, shoes, fancy jewelry, scepter (explain this item). At "GO," the first player in each team runs to the board to draw the first thing on the list. Then they race back and hand off the marker to the next player, who runs up to draw the next item. Give points for detail in drawing as well as finishing first. Replay with a king if desired.

Bible Story Replay

As a group, the children will retell the story of Esther. Have children stand in a circle. Give the three dress-ups to three of the children. Have them start retelling the story based on their characters. At your signal, the three should give their outfits to three others, who continue the story. Let those not using an outfit fill in the gaps or correct the story as needed. When done, the group should give a cheer for themselves!

ON THE FAST TRACK! *(Take-Home Papers)*

(Optional) Treasure box: **Who can remind us how to earn a prize from the treasure box? Yes! By taking this *On the Fast Track!* paper home, doing the activities, and memorizing the Bible verse. When you bring back the *Fast Track!* ticket signed next week, you'll get to choose a prize from the treasure box!** Show students the ticket.

Distribute the take-home papers just before children leave.

LESSON FOUR: The Talking Donkey

Memory Verse:
If you love me, you will obey what I command (John 14:15).

Bible Basis:
Numbers 22—23

Bible Truth:
We obey God when we pray.

Why do we pray?

You Will Need:

- [ ] 1 zip-bag of sugar cubes
- [ ] craft sticks
- [ ] play dough
- [ ] 1 poster board
- [ ] stick puppets of Balaam, donkey, messengers, and angel (Resources, 86-87)
- [ ] treat jar
- [ ] *Use the Clues!* bag and previous objects
- [ ] *On the Fast Track! #4* take-home paper
- [ ] *StationMaster Card #4*
- [ ] *(Optional)* treasure box
- [ ] *(Optional)* Snack: graham crackers, halved, or graham cracker stix, granola, napkins
- [ ] *(Optional)* Activity: craft sticks, pictures, markers, glue sticks

 When you see this icon, it means preparation will take more than five minutes.

 GET SET!
(Lesson Preparation)

- ■ 🕐 Print today's Bible memory verse on a poster board:
  If you love me, you will obey what I command (John 14:15).
  Hang the poster board at the front of the classroom.
- ■ Print "We obey God when we pray" on an index card and tape it to the zip-bag of sugar cubes.
- ■ 🕐 Enlarge the pictures of Balaam, donkey, messengers, and angel (see Resource Section) to full-page size. Color them, and glue them on craft sticks.
- ■ Make a copy of *On the Fast Track! #4* take-home paper for each child.
- ■ Make a copy of *StationMaster Card #4* for each helper.
- ■ Set out the treat jar, *Use the Clues!* bag and previous objects, and *(optional)* treasure box.
- ■ Set up snack or outside play activities if you use these in your children's ministry.

Play Dough Recipe

- ■ *2 c. flour*
- ■ *1 c. salt*
- ■ *4 T. cream of tartar*
- ■ *1 pkg. unsweetened dry drink mix for scent and color*
- ■ *2 c. warm water*
- ■ *2 T. cooking oil*

Stir over medium heat until mixture pulls away from sides to form a ball. Store in airtight container.
(for 8 to 10 children)

TICKETS PLEASE!
(Welcome and Bible Connection)

■ **Objective:** *To excite children's interest and connect their own experiences with the Bible Truth, children make play dough figures of Bible story characters.*

Welcome Time Activity: Play Dough

■ **Materials:** *purchased or homemade play dough*

As children arrive, give them a glob of play dough. Challenge them to make a donkey, a king, or angel first, then they may make what they choose. Ask if they know any stories that have a donkey, a king, and an angel. You can let the creations remain until after class, or have children put the play dough away when class begins.

Welcome the children and offer them a treat from the treat jar. Say: **Obeying God brings rewards. God rewards obedience with blessings. You're here today to learn how <u>praying is obeying God</u>. So take a sweet treat as a reward.** Children may finish their treat now, or set it aside to take home later.

(Optional) If children returned a signed *Fast Track!* ticket, they may choose a prize from the treasure box also.

Sharing Time and Bible Connection

Introduce the lesson by discussing the following questions with your students in the large group. As you talk, give every child the opportunity to say something.

■ **What does it mean to obey?** (do what you're told, follow someone's instructions)
■ **What happened the last time you obeyed a parent or teacher?** Let children share experiences.
■ **What happened when you didn't do what you should have done?** Allow sharing.

After sharing time, help your students connect their experiences to the Bible story from Numbers 22 and 23:

God wants us to obey and He rewards us when we do. Sometimes He has to discipline us for not obeying. In today's Bible story, you'll meet someone who wasn't sure he wanted to obey God, and learn what happened when he prayed about his choice. He found out that <u>praying is part of obeying God</u>. Let's get the whole story right now.

ALL ABOARD FOR BIBLE TRUTH!

Numbers 22–23

(Bible Discover and Learn Time)

- **Objective:** *Children will study Numbers 22 and 23 and hear that Balaam prayed and obeyed God.*
- **Materials:** *Stick puppets of Balaam, donkey, messengers, and angel*

Hold up the donkey puppet. **Hi, do you know what kind of animal I am?** Allow responses. **Yes, I'm a donkey, and this is my master, Balaam.** Hold up Balaam puppet. **Our story takes place long, long ago—before Jesus was even born.**

When Joshua led God's people into the promised land, my master was already there. Show Balaam again. **He was not one of God's people, but he knew God's voice.**

Many of the kings in the land were very afraid of Joshua and God's people, Israel, because God had done incredible things for them. Put Balaam and the donkey in one hand and the messengers in the other. **One of the kings was so afraid that he sent messengers to Balaam and asked him to put a curse on Israel.** Move messengers to Balaam. **Balaam asked God about that and God told him not to do it because the Israelites were blessed.**

The messengers returned to the king (move messengers to the king) **but the king did not like that answer. So, he sent the messengers to Balaam again** (move messengers back to Balaam) **and promised him a lot of presents and money.**

What would Balaam do, I wondered. Let children speculate briefly. **I'm sorry to say that the next morning, Balaam saddled me up and we went with the king's people.** Move Balaam and donkey to one hand; "walk" them together. **Bump, bump, bump. It was a long walk. Suddenly, I saw a terrifying sight! It was the angel of the Lord standing in the road with his sword drawn.** Hold up angel. **I was so frightened that I ran off the road into a field.** Put down angel. **Balaam couldn't see the angel so he beat me** (have Balaam "hit" the donkey) **for running away, and made me go back on the road. On we went.**

After a while, we came to a narrow path with rock walls on both sides. Uh-oh! There was the angel again! Hold up angel. **I was scared silly! I tried to get out of his way and squeezed up against the rocks.** Put down angel. **I was sorry that I crushed Balaam's foot, but he beat me again anyway.** Have Balaam hit the donkey. **I was not having a good day. But we kept going.**

Suddenly the angel was back in the road. Hold up angel. **We were in such a tight place I couldn't turn to the right or left. What should I do—obey my master and get us both killed? Or run away from the angel and make my master even angrier at me?** Put angel down.

I didn't know what to do, so I lay down, right there in the road. Boy, was Balaam mad! He began to hit me with his staff. Have Balaam hit the donkey.

That was enough! God gave me a voice like a human and I said (wiggle the donkey puppet), **"Why are you hitting me? What have I done wrong?"**

Balaam answered (wiggle the Balaam puppet), **"You have made me so angry that if I had a sword I would kill you right now!"**

I replied (wiggle the donkey puppet), **"Haven't I always been a good, obedient donkey to you? Have I ever done anything like this to you before?"**

Balaam said, **"No."** But then God opened his eyes (put Balaam and the donkey in one hand) **and he was able to see the angel of the Lord too.** Hold up angel. **Balaam fell down, frightened, just like me. God said, "If your donkey hadn't turned away, the angel would have killed you." I was proud. From then on, Balaam promised to do only what God wanted.** Put all figures down.

Balaam learned the hard way that God wanted him to obey, didn't he? God wants you to obey Him too. Hold up Balaam. **Did Balaam want to obey God?** (no) **But when Balaam talked to God, God used a donkey** (hold up donkey) **to make him obey.** Put down all figures.

God has told us to pray to Him. That's one reason why we pray. <u>We obey God when we pray</u>.

Use the Clues!
(Bible Review)

Okay, let's see what you remember about prayer. Bring out the *Use the Clues!* bag. Pull the yellow ball out of bag. **Think back to our Bible story from the first week. What does this clue remind us about prayer?** Have children raise their hands. Call on volunteers to name the story and the Bible Truth. (Refer to page 84 for a list of the clues, stories, and prayer truths they represent.) In the same way, review all the other objects from previous lessons.

■ **In today's story, what was Balaam's problem?** (a king wanted him to curse the Israelites, but God said no)

■ **What happened when Balaam thought about not obeying God?** (God got his attention by sending an angel with a sword)

■ **How did Balaam learn that <u>praying would help him obey</u>?** (God used his donkey to talk to him)

■ **What should you do when you're not sure if you will obey?** (talk to God and remember that He blesses us when we pray and obey)

When you're deciding whether you'll obey, you can talk to God about it. He helps us <u>obey when we pray</u> and listen to Him. That's what Balaam found out.

Show the bag of sugar cubes. **Donkeys like to eat sugar cubes, so these sugar cubes will remind us that <u>we obey God when we pray</u>.** Have children turn to a friend and say, "We obey God when we pray." Put the bag of sugar in the *Use the Clues!* bag.

BIBLE MEMORY WAYPOINT!

(Scripture Memory)

John 14:15

■ *Objective: Children will hide God's Word in their hearts for guidance, protection, and encouragement.*

Read the memory verse from the poster. Point to each word as you read it:

If you love me, you will obey what I command (John 14:15).

To help children memorize this week's Bible verse, have everyone hold up a hand like a puppet. They should open and close their thumbs to "say" the words:

If you love me, *(have the hand puppet kiss your cheek)*
you will obey *(have the hand puppet nod)*
what I command. *(have the hand puppet move like it's walking in front of you)*
(John 14:15)

Repeat the memory verse with puppetlike actions to help the children become familiar with the memory verse. Do it as a whole group, then children can work in pairs or small groups to say the verse to each other with the motions.

PRAYER STATION

■ *Objective: Children will explore and practice prayer for themselves.*
■ *Materials: Copies of* StationMaster Card #4 *for each helper*

Break into groups of three to five children. Assign a teen or adult helper to each group and give each helper a copy of *StationMaster Card #4* (see Resources).

SNACK STOP: ROCKY ROADS (Optional)

If you plan to provide a snack, this is an ideal time to serve it.

■ *Materials: graham crackers, halved, or graham cracker stix, granola, napkins*

Let children create a rocky road hemmed in with walls like Balaam and his donkey traveled. On a napkin, each child should lay strips of graham crackers end to end in two rows to be the rocky walls along the road. Add granola between the "walls" as the rocky road. Then eat. Talk about Balaam, his donkey, and how we obey when we pray.

Note: Always be aware of children with food allergies and have another option on hand if necessary.

APPLICATION

■ **Objective:** *Children will have opportunities to show how the lesson works in their own lives through activities and take-home papers.*

Some children's ministries may allow children to play outside at this point. If yours does not, choose one of the following activities.

Obstacle Course

Balaam and his donkey had a rough trip. Create an obstacle course for children to navigate. Use chairs to walk around, tables to crawl under, a narrow path between chair backs, and objects to step over. Have children go through the course in different modes, such as walking backward, in pairs, and skipping.

Puppet Productions

Provide craft sticks and smaller pictures of Balaam, the donkey, the messengers, and the angel for the children to color and cut out. These can be glued to the ends of the craft sticks and then used as puppets. Have children retell the story of Balaam and his donkey.

ON THE FAST TRACK! *(Take-Home Papers)*

(Optional) Treasure box: **Who can remind us how to earn a prize from the treasure box? Yes! By taking this *On the Fast Track!* paper home, doing the activities, and memorizing the Bible verse. When you bring back the *Fast Track!* ticket signed by a parent or another adult next week, you'll get to choose a prize from the treasure box!** Show students the ticket.

Distribute the take-home papers just before children leave.

Memory Verse:

I will listen to what God the Lord will say; he promises peace to his people (Psalm 85:8).
Note: Early elementary verse in **bold** *type.*

Bible Basis:

John 11:41-42; 17:1; Mark 1:10-11; Luke 22: 41-42; John 5:19

Bible Truth:

We pray because prayer is conversation with God.

What is prayer?

You Will Need:

- [ ] puppets
- [ ] toy telephone
- [ ] masking tape
- [ ] 3 poster boards
- [ ] treat jar
- [ ] *Use the Clues!* bag and previous objects
- [ ] *On the Fast Track! #5* take-home paper
- [ ] *StationMaster Card #5*
- [ ] *(Optional)* treasure box
- [ ] *(Optional)* Snack: red apple wedges (core removed), caramel spread, peanut butter or canned frosting, mini-marshmallows, plastic knives
- [ ] *(Optional)* Activity: masking tape or rope

 When you see this icon, it means preparation will take more than five minutes.

 ## GET SET!
(Lesson Preparation)

- ■ Print today's Bible memory verse on a poster board. Use markers of two colors, so the verse is divided into phrases (red: **"I will listen to what God the Lord will say"**; blue: **"He promises peace to His people"**). Hang the poster board at the front of the classroom.
- ■ Print "Prayer is conversation with God" on paper. Tape it to a play telephone.
- ■ Draw a huge mouth on a poster board and tape to one wall. Draw a huge ear on another board and tape to an opposite wall.
- ■ Make a copy of *On the Fast Track #5* take-home paper for each child.
- ■ Make a copy of *StationMaster Card #5* for each helper.
- ■ Set out the treat jar, *Use the Clues!* bag, and *(optional)* treasure box.
- ■ Set up snack or outside play activities if you use these in your children's ministry.

TICKETS PLEASE!
(Welcome and Bible Connection)

- ■ *Objective: To excite children's interest and connect their own experiences with the Bible Truth, children will "talk and listen" with puppets.*

Welcome Time Activity: Puppet Talk and Listen

- **Materials:** *Puppets*

Set out all puppets you have available, including homemade sock puppets or paper bag puppets. As children arrive, they may choose a puppet and "talk" to another student's puppet. If they don't know what to talk about, have them tell about a birthday party they went to, a family vacation, or what they like to do on Saturdays.

Welcome children as they arrive and offer them a treat from the treat jar. Say: **It feels so good to talk with someone you care about. That's how God feels about talking to you. Talking together is a sweet thing. Because you came to learn about talking to God today, enjoy a piece of candy.** Children may finish their treat now, or set it aside to take home later.

(Optional) If children returned a signed *Fast Track!* ticket, they may choose a prize from the treasure box also.

Sharing Time and Bible Connection

Introduce today's lesson by discussing these questions with the group. Give each child the opportunity to say something.

- **How many people have you talked to so far today?**
- **How many people talked to you today?**
- **Do you think praying is about talking to God or listening to God?**

Now help your students connect their discussion to the Bible story from the Gospels:

God is always so happy when you talk to Him. That's part of praying. But there's another part—*listening* to God talk! When you have a conversation with someone, both of you talk and both of you listen. That's how prayer is too. <u>We pray because we want to talk and listen to God</u>. There's a perfect example of someone who talked and listened to God. Who do you think that example is? Let's find out.

ALL ABOARD FOR BIBLE TRUTH!
(Bible Discover and Learn Time)

John 11:41-42; 17:1; Mark 1:10-11;
Luke 22:41-42; John 5:19

- **Objective:** *Children will discover that Jesus talked and listened to God the Father.*
- **Materials:** *poster of ear, poster of mouth, masking tape, Bible (bookmarked at John 11:41-42; 17:1; Mark 1:10-11; Luke 22:41-42; John 5:19), toy telephone*

Today you're going to be part of the Bible lesson. Instead of one story, I'm going to read to you five different parts of the Bible. Your job is to listen to each short section of verses and decide whether it's about *listening* or *talking*. If it's listening, you should go stand by the wall that has the big ear. Point to the ear poster. **If it's about talking, go to the mouth.** Point to mouth poster.

All these Bible sections are about the same person talking or listening. You'll find out who it is when I read them. Let's start. Listen to the whole section, but don't move to the ear or the mouth until I stop reading. Each time, after all the children have chosen a poster, ask for volunteers to explain why they made that choice. Affirm or correct their choice as needed. Children should return to their places in the story area for the next Scripture portion.

Read John 11:41-42: **"Then Jesus looked up and said, 'Father, I thank you that you have heard me. I knew that you always hear me, but I said this for the benefit of the people standing here, that they may believe that you sent me.'"** Children should move to the mouth poster. After volunteers explain their choices, children return to their places.

Read John 17:1: **"After Jesus said this, he looked toward heaven and prayed: 'Father, the time has come. Glorify your Son, that your Son may glorify you.'"** Children should move to the mouth poster. After volunteers explain their choices, children return to their places.

Read Mark 1:10-11: **"As Jesus was coming up out of the water, he saw heaven being torn open and the Spirit descending on him like a dove. And a voice came from heaven: 'You are my Son, whom I love; with you I am well pleased.'"** Children should move to the ear poster. After volunteers explain their choices, children return to you.

Read Luke 22:41-42: **"He withdrew about a stone's throw beyond them, knelt down and prayed, 'Father, if you are willing, take this cup from me; yet not my will, but yours be done.'"** Children should move to the mouth poster. After volunteers explain their choices, children return to you.

Read John 5:19: **"Jesus gave them this answer: 'I tell you the truth, the Son can do nothing by himself; he can do only what he sees his Father doing, because whatever the Father does the Son also does.'"** Children should move to the mouth poster. After volunteers explain their choices, children return to you.

Use the Clues
(Bible Review)

■ **In our lesson today, who was talking in each of those Bible verses?** (Jesus)

■ **Did He talk or did He listen?** (He did both)

■ **Who did Jesus talk to?** (God the Father)

■ **How did Jesus show He was listening to God the Father?** (He didn't do all the talking, He did what God said to do)

■ **What kinds of things did Jesus say when He talked to God?** (He thanked God, He asked God for something, He wanted God to be glorified)

■ **How can we be like Jesus when He prayed to the Father?** (we can choose to <u>pray and have a conversation with God</u>)

Jesus prayed by talking and listening to God. He had a conversation with God. That's why we pray—to have a conversation with our heavenly Father. We can do as Jesus did by talking to God and also by listening to Him. **God loves to hear from us, and sometimes He also wants us to listen to what He has to tell us. We talk and we listen.**

Show the toy telephone. **You all know that you don't need a phone to talk to God! But this telephone is the perfect symbol of having a conversation. Who's talked on the phone this week?** Let children respond. **You already know that on the phone you talk and you listen. When you see a telephone, you can remember that we pray because we're having a <u>conversation with God</u>.** Set the telephone aside and bring out the *Use the Clues!* bag with objects from previous lessons.

Now, let's review what we've learned about prayer other weeks. Have volunteers pull an object from the bag and try to remember the story and prayer truth. (On page 84 you'll find the objects, story, and prayer truth they represent.) Add the telephone to the bag when you are finished.

BIBLE MEMORY WAYPOINT!
(Scripture Memory)

Psalm 85:8

■ *Objective: Children will hide God's Word in their hearts for guidance, protection, and encouragement.*

Read this week's memory verse from the two-color poster. Point to each word as you read it:

"I will listen to what God the LORD will say; he promises peace to his people" (Psalm 85:8).

To help children memorize the verse, break them two groups. Arrange the groups so they face each other in two lines, shoulder to shoulder. Group 1 will say the first phrase denoted by one color, which group 2 will echo. Group 1 will say the next phrase (a different color), with group 2 echoing again. Continue through the verse. After a couple of times through the verse, give the children in group 1 balls or beanbags. As they say their phrase, they'll toss the toy to the person across from them. As group 2 echoes, they'll toss the toys back. Repeat, with children speaking faster.

PRAYER STATION

- ■ **Objective:** *Children will explore and practice prayer for themselves.*
- ■ **Materials:** *Copies of* StationMaster Card #5 *for each helper*

Divide the class into groups of three to five children. Assign a teen or adult helper to each small group and give each helper a copy of *StationMaster Card #5* (see Resources).

SNACK STOP: MARSHMALLOW MOUTHS (Optional)

If you plan to provide a snack, this is an ideal time to serve it.

- ■ **Materials:** *red apple wedges (core removed), caramel spread, peanut butter or ready-made frosting, mini-marshmallows, plastic knives*

Children can spread frosting or another creamy filling on one apple wedge and lay a second on top to make two lips. The mini-marshmallows can be pushed into the frosting as teeth. As children create and eat their snack, engage them in conversation about their everyday lives.

Note: Always be aware of children with food allergies and have another option on hand if necessary.

APPLICATION

- ■ **Objective:** *Children will have opportunities to show how the lesson works in their own lives through activities and take-home papers.*

Some children's ministries may allow children to play outside at this point. If yours does not, choose one of the following activities.

Talk or Listen

Lay a rope or tape a line on the floor in the playing area. Have children line up facing you at one end, on one side of the line. Tell them that they're standing on the "talk" side. When you say "talk" they should jump to that side. If they're already there, they stay there. If you say "listen" they jump over the line to the "listen" side, or stay there if they're already there. Give the commands "talk" and "listen" in random order, sometimes repeating the same one. Children will have to hop sideways back and forth over the line. Those who don't go when they should, or go when they shouldn't are out.

Telephone

Play the classic game "Telephone." Children sit in a circle (make more than one if you have a large group) and pass a sentence or phrase around the circle. You'll whisper the message in one child's ear and that child whispers it to the one next to him. The message continues around the circle until the last child receives it and then speaks it out loud. See how it changes from the start to the end!

ON THE FAST TRACK! *(Take-Home Papers)*

(Optional) Treasure box: **Who can remind us how to earn a prize from the treasure box? Yes! By taking this *On the Fast Track!* paper home, doing the activities, and memorizing the Bible verse. When you bring back the *Fast Track!* ticket signed by a parent or another adult next week, you'll get to choose a prize from the treasure box!** Show students the ticket.

Distribute the take-home papers just before children leave.

Memory Verse:

Your kingdom come, your will be done on earth as it is in heaven (Matthew 6:10).

Bible Basis:

1 Kings 18:21-39

Bible Truth:

We pray according to God's will.

How do we pray?

You Will Need:

- [ ] Bible time dress-up box
- [ ] ball
- [ ] 1 zip-bag containing three rocks
- [ ] 1 poster board
- [ ] play dough, enough so each child can make three stones, each two inches in diameter
- [ ] 1 pitcher of water
- [ ] 1/2 sheet red construction or flash paper
- [ ] 1 shallow baking dish
- [ ] toy bowling pins or empty 2-liter plastic bottles
- [ ] treat jar
- [ ] *Use the Clues!* bag and previous objects
- [ ] *On the Fast Track! #6* take-home paper
- [ ] *StationMaster Card #6*
- [ ] *(Optional)* treasure box
- [ ] *(Optional)* Snack: mini-marshmallows, miniature graham cracker creatures
- [ ] *(Optional)* Activity: 1 ball of yarn

GET SET!

(Lesson Preparation)

- ▪ Print today's Bible memory verse on a poster board:
  Your kingdom come, your will be done on earth as it is in heaven (Matthew 6:10).
  Hang the poster board at the front of the classroom.
- ▪ Print "We pray to know God's will" on an index card, and tape it to the zip-bag of rocks.
- ▪ Cut the construction or flash paper into flames so they can be set on an altar.
- ▪ Make a copy of *On the Fast Track! #6* take-home paper for each child.
- ▪ Make a copy of *StationMaster Card #6* for each helper.
- ▪ Set out treat jar, *Use the Clues!* bag and previous objects, and *(optional)* treasure box.
- ▪ Set up snack or outside play activities if you use these in your children's ministry.

When you see this icon, it means preparation will take more than five minutes.

TICKETS PLEASE!
(Welcome and Bible Connection)

■ **Objective:** *To excite children's interest and connect their own experiences with the Bible Truth, children will play a bowling game and talk about true and false prophets.*

Welcome Time Activity: Prophet Bowling

■ **Materials:** *toy bowling pins or empty 2-liter plastic bottles, ball*

As children arrive, let them play "Prophet Bowling." The plastic bottle "pins" can be set up in a tight formation by some of the children while one player takes a turn trying to knock them down by rolling the ball from several feet away (make distances longer for older kids). While you are playing, talk with children about what a true prophet is (a person who gives messages from God) and explain that in today's story there are false prophets and we're bowling them over!

When everyone has arrived, welcome children and offer them a treat from the treat jar. Say: **God likes it when children come and talk to Him. Whenever they do, He rewards them with His presence. The treats remind us of that reward.** Children may finish their treat now, or set it aside to take home later.

(Optional) If children returned a signed *Fast Track!* ticket, they may choose a prize from the treasure box also.

Sharing Time and Bible Connection

Introduce today's lesson by discussing the following questions with your students in the large group. As you talk, give every child the opportunity to say something.

■ **Do you think you can read people's minds and know what they want?** (no)
■ **How do you know what your parents want you to do?** (they tell you)
■ **How can you know what God wants you to do?** (pray and ask Him)
■ **How does God tell you what He wants you to do?** (He answers your prayer; His Word, the Bible, tells us; your parents or teacher or pastor teach you)

Help students connect their discussion to the Bible story they're about to hear from 1 Kings 18:

God knows we can't read His mind. One reason He wants us to pray is so we can understand what He wants us to do. God shows us what to do because we pray. Sometimes knowing what God wants us to do is called knowing God's will. Have you heard that before? We don't have to guess or try to read God's mind. <u>We can pray to know God's will</u>. The Bible story today is an amazing example of how someone prayed to know what God wanted. Let's learn more about it.

ALL ABOARD FOR BIBLE TRUTH!   1 Kings 18:21-39
(Bible Discover and Learn Time)

- ■ *Objective:* Children will study 1 Kings 18 and hear that Elijah prayed to find out God's will.
- ■ *Materials:* play dough, 1 zip-bag with three rocks in it, construction or flash paper flames, pitcher of water, shallow baking dish

When you tell the story, use different voices for the different characters. Be dramatic and emphatic to bring the story alive.

Hand a lump of play dough to each child. **While I tell the story, you can make three round rocks from your play dough.**

Have you heard of Elijah? Accept responses. **He was a prophet in the Old Testament whose job was to give the people of Israel messages from God. He knew God really well because he talked to God a lot.**

One day, God said to Elijah, "Go tell King Ahab I'm really angry at him. He worships false gods instead of the one true God." Whoa. Elijah knew this was really serious. Worshiping false gods was a terrible thing. So off Elijah went to see the king. How do you think Ahab felt about Elijah's message from God? Let children respond. **Ahab was not at all pleased. In fact, he was mad, mad, mad! This is not a good thing in a king. But <u>Elijah had prayed and he knew what God wanted</u> next. So he told King Ahab, "Tell 450 prophets of your god, Baal, to come to Mount Carmel." Elijah was planning a showdown! It would be the 450 prophets of Baal and one prophet of the true God, face-to-face.**

When the 450 prophets of Baal got to Mount Carmel, there was Elijah—alone! A big crowd of people had shown up to see what would happen. Everyone wanted to know which God was most powerful. Elijah told the people, "You can't keep switching gods. If the Lord is really God, follow Him; but if Baal is god, then follow him." Ooh. Strong words!

Then Elijah said, "Let's have a test. Let's get two bulls and cut them up to be sacrificed. We'll put the bull meat on the wood to be burned, but . . . we won't set it on fire. Then you prophets call to your god, Baal. And I'll call on my God. Whoever answers by sending down a flaming fire to burn the sacrifice is the one true God."

All the people agreed this was a great idea.

Have children bring their rocks up and make two stacks. One will be Baal's altar. The second altar should be built in a shallow baking pan. Thank children for helping.

Elijah let the prophets of Baal go first. They prepared their sacrifice. Then they prayed to their god, Baal, to send down fire and burn up the sacrifice. No answer. They called out to Baal all morning long: "O Baal, answer us!" But nothing happened. They even danced around the altar they had made.

Elijah yelled, "Shout louder. Maybe he's on a trip or busy doing something else!" Elijah was making fun of their god. Ha, ha, ha, ha, ha! Those prophets wore themselves out trying to get Baal to send fire. By

evening, still nothing had happened. **Why do you think nothing happened?** (because the prophets believed in a false god)

Now it was Elijah's turn. He knew what would happen. <u>He had prayed and he knew God's will</u>. Elijah rebuilt the altar and dug a ditch around it. He put the sacrifice on the wood. Then Elijah did a crazy thing. **He had water poured on top of the sacrifice!** *Pour water from a pitcher over Elijah's altar in the pan.*

Elijah prayed, "Dear Lord, let everyone know today that You are the one true God and that I have done everything that You commanded me to do." *Place the red paper on top of the altar.* **Whoosh! God sent a big flame of fire right down onto the sacrifice. It was so hot, the people probably felt like they were baking. The fire of the Lord fell and burned up the sacrifice. Not only that, the fire burned the wood, the stones, the soil, and all the *water* in the ditch.** *Knock the stones over so that children cannot see them in the bottom of the baking dish, as if the fire consumed them.*

What do you think all the people did? *Let children respond.* **They bowed down and worshiped the one true God!** <u>Elijah knew what God wanted him to do because he prayed</u>.

Use the Clues!
(Bible Review)

- **In our lesson today, how did Elijah find out what God wanted?** (he prayed)
- **What did God want Elijah to do?** (tell King Ahab to stop worshiping false gods)
- **How did Elijah cause fire to come down on his sacrifice?** (he prayed)
- **What happened when Elijah put the prophets of Baal to the test to see which god was powerful?** (the prophets of Baal didn't get their god to do anything, but the real God burned up the whole sacrifice and altar)
- **How can we know God's will for us?** (we need to pray and ask Him)
- **What is something you need to know God's will about?** *Let children respond or just ponder.*

Elijah knew God would tell him what He wanted Elijah to do. How did he know? Because he talked to God a lot and trusted God would answer him. We might not feel as confident as Elijah, but God still tells us what He wants if we're willing to ask. It's like knowing that you need to help out at home, so you ask your mom or dad what they want you to do. They usually tell you, don't they? That's just like it is with God. *Show the children the bag of three rocks with the card "We pray to know God's will" attached.* **Rocks! That's our reminder today!** *Have children pass the bag around and read the card. Then set it aside.* **The rocks are our reminder that <u>we can pray to know God's will</u>. He'll tell us!** *Bring out the Use the Clues! bag with objects from previous lessons.*

Now, let's review what we've learned about prayer other weeks. *Have volunteers pull an object from the bag and try to remember the story and prayer truth. (On page 84 you'll find the objects, story, and prayer truth they represent.) Add the zip-bag of rocks to the bag when you are finished.*

BIBLE MEMORY WAYPOINT!
(Scripture Memory)

Matthew 6:10

- ■ **Objective:** *Children will hide God's Word in their hearts for guidance, protection, and encouragement.*

Read memory verse from the poster, pointing to each word as you read it:
Your kingdom come, your will be done on earth as it is in heaven (Matthew 6:10).
   To help children memorize this verse, divide them into two groups. One group will make rap noises while another comes up with the right rhythm to say the words. When you've finished experimenting, put the words and noises together and have the whole class rap it a few times to help children become more familiar with the verse. If possible, let the children perform the rap for parents when class is over.

PRAYER STATION

- ■ **Objective:** *Children will explore and practice prayer for themselves.*
- ■ **Materials:** *Copies of* StationMaster Card #6 *for each helper*

Break into groups of three to five children. Assign one teen or adult helper per group and give each helper a copy of *StationMaster Card #6* (see Resources).

SNACK STOP: PROPHETS AND ALTARS (Optional)

If you plan to provide a snack, this is an ideal time to serve it.

- ■ **Materials:** *mini-marshmallows, miniature graham cracker animals*

Have children build a small altar with some mini-marshmallows, then use some graham cracker "people" to simulate the story before devouring the scene.
   Note: Always be aware of children with food allergies and have another option on hand if necessary.

APPLICATION

■ *Objective:* *Children will have opportunities to show how the lesson works in their own lives through activities and take-home papers.*

Some children's ministries may allow children to play outside at this point. If yours does not, choose one of the following activities.

Tightrope Walking

Sometimes learning to do God's will is like walking on a tightrope: the more you listen, the better you become. Unroll a ball of yarn and lay it on the floor so that it crisscrosses itself loosely around the room. Let each child stand somewhere on the yarn. They'll follow the yarn until they get back to where they started. Impress on them that following the yarn is like walking in God's will; it takes your constant attention. If two children meet, they must find a way to walk around one another without stepping off the yarn.

Rappin' the Word

Have the children review the memory verse by rehearsing their rap. They can also perform it as two groups that say the lines back and forth to each other. Let the children perform the rap for parents who come to collect their children.

ON THE FAST TRACK! *(Take-Home Papers)*

(Optional) Treasure box: **Here's your *On the Fast Track!* paper to take home. You can do the activities and learn a Bible verse to earn a prize next week. Just have your parents or another adult sign the *Fast Track!* ticket and bring it back next week to get to choose something from the treasure box!**

Distribute the take-home papers just before children leave.

LESSON SEVEN: Great Faith Heals a Servant

How do we pray?

Memory Verse:
And without faith it is impossible to please God (Hebrews 11:6).

Bible Basis:
Luke 7:1-10

Bible Truth:
We pray with faith that God is in control.

You Will Need:

- [ ] Bible time dress-up box
- [ ] an empty medicine bottle
- [ ] 1 poster board
- [ ] 6 balloons
- [ ] 6 strips of paper, 4 inches in length
- [ ] 3 adults to share brief stories about God answering their prayers
- [ ] illustration of the sick servant (Resources, 85)
- [ ] treat jar
- [ ] *Use the Clues!* bag and previous objects
- [ ] *On the Fast Track! #7* take-home paper
- [ ] *StationMaster Card #7*
- [ ] (Optional) treasure box
- [ ] (Optional) Snack: pretzels

When you see this icon, it means preparation will take more than five minutes.

GET SET!
(Lesson Preparation)

- ■ 🕐 Print today's Bible memory verse on a poster board. Spell the word FAITH in *capital letters*:
  And without faith it is impossible to please God (Hebrews 11:6).
  Hang the poster board at the front of the classroom.
- ■ 🕐 On each strip of paper, write one or two words of the Bible verse, so that you have six segments (including the reference). Roll the papers up and insert inside the six balloons, then inflate and tie the balloons.
- ■ Make a copy of *On the Fast Track! #7* take-home paper for each child.
- ■ Make a copy of *StationMaster Card #7* for each helper.
- ■ Set out the treat jar, *Use the Clues!* bag, and (optional) treasure box.

TICKETS PLEASE!
(Welcome and Bible Connection)

- ■ *Objective: To excite children's interest and connect their own experiences with the Bible Truth, children will play a game in which they are following the commands of a "master."*

Welcome Time Activity: The Master Says

While you're waiting for all the children to arrive, play an adaptation of "Simon Says" by substituting the words "The Master Says" before the commands. One child can start as the "Master" giving commands such as touch the floor, turn around, kick up your feet, etc. When a command isn't prefaced with "The Master says" the players shouldn't follow the command. Those that do should step out. Change "masters" after six or eight commands. Talk to children about what a master is. Tell them today's Bible story is about a master who had faith in Jesus.

When everyone has arrived, welcome the children and offer them a treat from the treat jar. Say: **God is pleased to reward us when we come to learn about and talk to Him. Enjoy a treat the way God enjoys your being with Him.** Children may finish their treat now, or set it aside to take home later.

(Optional) If children returned a signed *Fast Track!* ticket, they may choose a prize from the treasure box also.

Sharing Time and Bible Connection

Introduce today's lesson by discussing the following questions with your students in the large group. As you talk, give every child the opportunity to say something.

- **Can you remember a time you were sick?**
- **When have you prayed to Jesus and He's answered your prayer?**
- **When have you prayed for Jesus to heal someone who's been sick?**

Now help your students connect their discussion to the Bible story from Luke 7:1-10:

No one likes to be sick. Sometimes doctors can't help a sick person. But there's always Someone who can help—Jesus! He wants us to talk to Him when we have a need. Jesus says when we believe He can help us and we pray about it, He will answer our prayers. Let find out about how Jesus answered when someone <u>prayed with faith</u>.

ALL ABOARD FOR BIBLE TRUTH!   Luke 7:1-10
(Bible Discover and Learn Time)

- *Objective: Children will study Luke 7:1-10 and hear that because of the centurion's faith Jesus healed his servant.*
- *Materials: Bible time dress-up box, an empty medicine bottle*

Today I need some puppets to help tell the Bible story. Hmm, I have no puppets. What shall I do? I know! Some of you will be my puppets! Choose eight older children and help them find appropriate clothing from the dress-up box. You will need a Jesus, soldier, sick servant, two messengers, and three friends. Station the centurion, elders, friends, and sick servant on one side of the room and Jesus on the other side. Have the sick servant lie on the ground and look sick. The centurion, elders, and friends will stand around the sick servant. You might want to practice a few times before starting.

Open your Bible and lay it on the table or your lap during the story. Use expressive voices for the different characters.

First we need to find out what a centurion is. Does anyone know? Take answers and affirm the right one: a soldier. **Now in today's story from Luke, Jesus had been traveling. He was in the town of Capernaum. In that town, a centurion's servant was sick and about to die. The centurion, who was the servant's master, really liked this servant. He had heard about Jesus, so** (place centurion's hand up to his ear) **he sent some messengers to Him.**

Touch the centurion's shoulder. **"Go get Jesus. He can heal my servant."** Touch the centurion's shoulder again.

Move two messengers over to Jesus and touch their shoulders. **"Please come and heal the centurion's servant. The centurion is a good man."** Touch two messengers' shoulders.

Jesus said (touch Jesus' shoulder), **"I will come."** Touch Jesus' shoulder. **Jesus went with the messengers.** Move Jesus and messengers halfway across the room.

The little group wasn't far from the centurion's house when Jesus saw some people walking toward Him. They had another message for Jesus. These friends of the centurion told him (push friends to Jesus and then touch friends' shoulders), **"Lord, You don't need to come all the way here. I don't deserve to have You come to my house. I don't even consider myself worthy to come to You. If You just say the word, my servant will be healed. I understand You're in charge."** Touch three friends' shoulders. **The centurion believed that Jesus could heal his servant just by saying it. <u>That centurion had lots of faith in Jesus when he asked for help</u>.**

Wow! Jesus was amazed. He turned to his friends following Him and said (turn Jesus toward the rest of the class, and then touch Jesus' shoulder), **"This man has great faith in what God can do!"** Touch Jesus' shoulder. **"Go on back home," Jesus said to the centurion's friends.** Move the two friends back to the centurion.

So the friends turned around and went back. They could hardly believe what they found. Incredible! Amazing! A miracle! The servant was well! Jesus had healed him because <u>the centurion asked with faith</u>. Help the sick servant up. Touch his shoulder. **Now everyone could see that Jesus was in charge of everything. Having faith in Him gave the centurion's prayers power.**

Thank the "volunteers," let them put dress-up clothes away, and sit down.

Use the Clues!
(Bible Review)

As you discuss the following questions with your students, show them the illustration of the sick servant and the centurion (see Resources, 85).

- **What did the centurion do to help his sick servant?** (he sent friends to ask Jesus to make the servant well)
- **What did the centurion need so that Jesus would answer his need for help?** (faith) **What is faith?** (believing that Jesus could do what he asked)
- **What things do you want to ask God's help for?** Let each child share one thing.
- **When you pray, what do you need before God can answer you?** (when we pray, we need to have faith)

The centurion knew there was nothing he could do for his sick servant. But he completely believed that Jesus could make the servant well. He had faith and he asked Jesus for help. That's exactly what we can do. We pray with faith. Show the children the empty medicine bottle. **When you see this bottle, it can remind you that we pray with faith. Remember how the centurion believed Jesus would help when he asked Him.** Set the pill bottle aside and bring out the *Use the Clues!* bag with objects from previous lessons.

Now, let's review what we've learned about prayer from our other lessons. Have volunteers pull an object from the bag and try to remember the story and prayer truth. (On page 84 you'll find the objects, story, and prayer truth they represent.) Add the pill bottle to the bag when you are finished.

BIBLE MEMORY WAYPOINT!
(Scripture Memory)

Hebrews 11:6

- ***Objective:*** *Children will hide God's Word in their hearts for guidance, protection, and encouragement.*

Read the memory verse from the poster. Point to each word as you read it:
And without faith it is impossible to please God (Hebrews 11:6).

To help children memorize the Bible verse, divide the class into six groups. Give each group a balloon to burst in any way they choose. Inside they'll find a verse segment. One person from each group should hold their segment. Let students help you arrange the six verse holders into correct order. Then have the whole group repeat the verse. Have them start by whispering it, then grow in volume as they repeat the verse several times until they reach the loudest level you want them to use.

PRAYER STATION

- **Objective:** *Children will explore and practice prayer for themselves.*
- **Materials:** *Copies of* StationMaster Card #7 *for each helper*

Before breaking into prayer groups, ask three adults from your church to briefly talk (three minutes or less) to your children about how God has answered prayer in their lives. Then break into small groups of three to five children. Assign a teen or adult helper to each small group and give each helper a copy of *StationMaster Card #7* (see Resources Section) with ideas for group discussion and prayer.

SNACK STOP: FAITH STICKS (Optional)

If you plan to provide a snack, this an ideal time to serve it.

- **Materials:** *pretzel sticks, memory verse poster*

Highlight the word "faith" on the memory verse poster. Shake out a handful of pretzels for each child and have them spell FAITH with their pretzels. When they've spelled the word, they may eat the pretzels.

Note: Always be aware of children with food allergies and have another option on hand if necessary.

APPLICATION

- **Objective:** *Children will have opportunities to show how the lesson works in their own lives through activities and take-home papers.*

Some children's ministries may allow children to play outside at this point. If yours does not, choose one of the following activities.

Trust Me?

You'll need one adult or one adult helper for each group. A child should stand on the floor about two feet in front of the adult. The other children should stand in a line next to the adult. The adult should say, "Trust me?" If the child has enough faith that the adult and other children will catch her, she should fall backwards and be caught by each person in turn. Then the next child repeats the process. Once everyone has had a turn to catch and be caught, tell children that this game reminds us that having faith in God means we believe He can and will do what He says—even when we can't see Him!

Faith Cheer

Using the memory verse, have the children (in one large group or a few smaller groups) make up a cheer. They can use the exact words or paraphrase the verse, as long as the meaning is unchanged. Have groups perform their cheer for parents who pick them up.

 ON THE FAST TRACK! *(Take-Home Papers)*

(Optional) Treasure box: **Who can remind us how to earn a prize from the treasure box? Yes! By taking this** *On the Fast Track!* **paper home, doing the activities, and memorizing the Bible verse. When you bring back the** *Fast Track!* **ticket signed by a parent or another adult next week, you'll get to choose a prize from the treasure box!** Show students the ticket.

Distribute the take-home papers just before children leave.

LESSON EIGHT: God Wins a Big Battle

Memory Verse:
Call to me and I will answer you and tell you great and unsearchable things you do not know (Jeremiah 33:3).

Bible Basis:
2 Chronicles 20

Bible Truth:
We pray to ask God for what we need.

How do we pray?

You Will Need:

- [ ] butcher paper
- [ ] 1 poster board
- [ ] 6 sheets of paper
- [ ] Bible time dress-up box
- [ ] musical instrument, real or toy
- [ ] church prayer partners and pastors, one for each prayer group
- [ ] treat jar
- [ ] *Use the Clues!* bag and previous objects
- [ ] *On the Fast Track! #8* take-home paper
- [ ] *StationMaster Card #8*
- [ ] (Optional) treasure box
- [ ] (Optional) Snack: long party toothpicks; fruits in chunks (bananas, apples, grapes; avoid fruits associated with allergies, such as strawberries)
- [ ] (Optional) Activity: inflated balloons (1 per every 4–6 children), praise music, CD/tape player

When you see this icon, it means preparation will take more than five minutes.

GET SET!
(Lesson Preparation)

- ■ ⏱ Print today's Bible memory verse on a poster board:
  Call to me and I will answer you and tell you great and unsearchable things you do not know (Jeremiah 33:3).
  Hang the poster board at the front of the classroom.
- ■ Print each of these Bible texts on a separate slip of paper:
  Group 1: 2 Chronicles 20:3
  Group 2: 2 Chronicles 20:13
  Group 3: 2 Chronicles 20:18
  Group 4: 2 Chronicles 20:22
  Group 5: 2 Chronicles 20:24
  Group 6: 2 Chronicles 20:27
- ■ ⏱ Invite prayer partners and pastors to join your children's ministry during the prayer time this week.
- ■ Ask one prayer partner to speak for under five minutes about how God answered one of their prayers.
- ■ Tape a 10-foot length of butcher paper to a flat wall at children's eye level; set boxes of markers or crayons on the floor in front of it.
- ■ Make a copy of *On the Fast Track! #8* take-home paper for each child.
- ■ Make a copy of *StationMaster Card #8* for each helper.
- ■ Put the musical instrument in the *Use the Clues!* bag.
- ■ Set out treat jar and (optional) treasure box.
- ■ Set up snack or outside play activities if you use these in your children's ministry.

TICKETS PLEASE!
(Welcome and Bible Connection)

■ *Objective:* To excite children's interest and connect their own life experiences with the Bible Truth, children will make a mural and talk about the joy of God's blessing.

Welcome Time Activity: Musical Marching Mural

■ *Materials:* butcher paper, markers or crayons, tape

As children arrive, direct them to the wall where you have taped the butcher paper. Have your adult or teen helpers invite children to work together to create a mural of musicians playing all kinds of instruments that they might use in a marching band. Tell children in their Bible story today people were so happy to have God's blessing that they celebrated and played music!

When everyone has arrived, welcome the children and offer them a treat from the treat jar. Say: **God likes it when children come and talk to Him. When we ask God for His help, He blesses us. This treat is a reminder of God's blessings to us.** Children may finish their treat now, or set it aside to take home later.

(Optional) If children returned a signed *Fast Track!* ticket, they may choose a prize from the treasure box.

Sharing Time and Bible Connection

Introduce today's lesson by discussing these questions with the class, giving every child the opportunity to say something.

■ **What is something you asked for today or yesterday?**
■ **How do you feel when you receive something you asked for?** (good, happy, thankful)
■ **What is a blessing?** (something good God gives us or does for us)

Help your students connect their discussion to the Bible story from 2 Chronicles 20:

God wants to bless you. <u>He loves to hear our prayers because when He answers them He can bless us</u>. But the only way to receive these blessings is to ask Him in prayer for what we need. In the Old Testament, a king named Jehoshaphat had something really big to ask. He was afraid and his enemies were coming to attack him. <u>Did Jehoshaphat tell God what he needed and receive a blessing</u>? Let's find out what happened.

ALL ABOARD FOR BIBLE TRUTH!
(Bible Discover and Learn Time)

2 Chronicles 20

- ■ **Objective:** *Children will study 2 Chronicles 20 and hear that Jehoshaphat prayed when he needed help and God blessed him and his people.*
- ■ **Materials:** *Bible time dress-up box; papers with story segments on them; musical instrument, real or toy*

For today's story, we're all going to have a part. Divide the class into six groups, making sure some older children are in each group. Assign each group one of the Bible passages written on paper. Give the groups about four minutes to read their passage and choose how to make a freeze-frame dramatic interpretation of their passage. Explain that when you get to that part of the story, that group will create their freeze-frame. Each group may choose items from the dress-up box to enhance their frozen drama.

This story happens when Jehoshaphat was the king of Judah. Two enemy countries called Moab and Ammon decided to attack Judah. Messengers came dashing up to King Jehoshaphat: (huff and puff) **"A huge crowd of attackers is coming! They're already at En-gedi—they're almost here!"** Group 1's freeze-frame begins. They should hold this pose until it is group 2's turn. **Jehoshaphat was scared all the way to his toes. He knew he had to ask God's help. He called everyone in the country to fast and pray for God's help. People from all over came together to pray. It was a huge prayer meeting!**

King Jehoshaphat stood in front of the gigantic crowd. He prayed from his heart to God about what was happening. "God," he said, "You hold all the power and might in the entire world. No one can stand up against You. Now our enemies are coming to attack us! We need Your help, God. We can't fight these armies on our own. We're looking to see what You'll do for us." End first freeze-frame; begin group 2's freeze-frame.

All the people of Judah were standing, praying with Jehoshaphat to God. Grown-ups, kids, babies. Then God sent His spirit to a prophet named Jahaziel. You remember that a prophet is a person who brings a message from God. His message was, "Don't be afraid. This battle isn't yours, it's God's. Go out ready to fight, but don't do anything. Tomorrow just go out there and God will do it all." End this freeze-frame and have group 3 begin theirs.

Whew! The people were relieved. Jehoshaphat fell down to his knees and put his face to the ground. He wanted to honor God for giving His help. He could see that <u>God wanted to bless them because they had asked</u>. Every last person there worshiped God by kneeling down and putting their faces to the ground.

So the next morning Judah's armies knew exactly what to do. They put on their armor. They picked up their swords and bows and shields. And they went out to meet the enemy. Jehoshaphat reminded everyone of God's words. "Believe in God!" he shouted. Then he did something that seems kind of strange to us. End group 3's freeze-frame;

begin group 4. **Jehoshaphat put some singers up at the front of the soldiers. The singers started singing and praising God out loud.**

And then God went to work. He made an ambush against all the enemy armies. Guess what happened? They were all destroyed. The enemies even helped kill each other! End group 4's freeze-frame; begin group 5.

When Judah's armies got to the lookout point, they looked down and saw every last one of their enemies was dead. Not a single one had gotten away! The people went down to take all the weapons, clothes, jewels, and other valuable things from the enemies. They gathered goods for three days! Finally they were done. Then they all came together and thanked God for His help. End group 5's freeze-frame; begin the final freeze-frame of group 6.

It was time for a celebration. Jehoshaphat led everyone back to Jerusalem cheering and praising God. Full of excitement, they played their harps and blew their trumpets to let everyone know that their God was the greatest. End final freeze-frame and have children sit down.

Use the Clues!
(Bible Review)

■ **Why did Jehoshaphat need God's help?** (powerful enemy armies were coming to attack Judah)

■ **How did the king get God's help?** (he prayed and told God what he needed)

■ **How did God answer Jehoshaphat's prayer and bless Judah?** (by completely killing all the enemies)

■ **How can we follow Jehoshaphat's example?** (we need to ask God for help and then He can bless us)

■ **What kinds of things can we ask God's help for?** Let children offer their suggestions and affirm them.

When Judah was desperate and needed help fast, Jehoshaphat talked to God. He asked for help and God blessed Judah by killing every last enemy. Remember how the people showed God thanks? They praised Him and worshiped Him. When God blesses us, we should always be quick to thank Him and praise Him for His blessings.

Show the *Use the Clues!* bag. **What do you think is in the *Use the Clues!* bag this time?** After children guess a bit, take the musical instrument from the bag. **This instrument is a reminder that we can ask God for what we need.** Then they praised Him with singing and music.

Now let's review our other lessons about prayer. Bring out the objects from previous lessons. Have volunteers pull an object from the bag and try to remember the story and prayer truth. On page 84 you'll find the objects, story, and prayer truth they represent.

BIBLE MEMORY WAYPOINT!

Jeremiah 33:3

(Scripture Memory)

■ *Objective: Children will hide God's Word in their hearts for guidance, protection, and encouragement.*

Read the memory verse from the poster. Point to each word as you read it:

Call to me and I will answer you and tell you great and unsearchable things you do not know (Jeremiah 33:3).

Use an echo activity to help children memorize the verse. Form two groups, being sure some readers are in both groups. One group should speak a phrase and the other will echo it. Continue through the verse, phrase by phrase. Then switch groups. They can do the echo in different volumes, such as loud, whispers, or regular voices.

PRAYER STATION

■ *Objective: Children will explore and practice prayer for themselves.*
■ *Materials: Copies of* StationMaster Card #8 *for each pastor or prayer partner*

Introduce the prayer partners and pastors. Explain that they pray for the people in your church. Have one prayer partner or pastor talk for a few minutes about how God has answered prayer. Then break up the group into small groups of three to five children. Each group should be led by a prayer partner or pastor. Give each leader a copy of the *StationMaster Card #8* (see Resources) with ideas for discussion and prayer.

This is an ideal opportunity to let children respond personally to what they've learned about God through prayer. If you feel this is right for your group, use today's prayer time to encourage your students to commit their lives to Christ.

SNACK STOP: CELEBRATION STICKS (Optional)

If you plan to provide a snack, this is an ideal time to serve it.

■ *Materials: long party toothpicks; fruits in chunks (bananas, apples, grapes; avoid fruits associated with allergies, such as strawberries)*

Set out plates of fruits in chunks. Give each child two toothpicks and let them build their own fruit kabobs with three or four pieces of fruit.

APPLICATION

■ *Objective: Children will have opportunities to show how the lesson works in their own lives through activities and take-home papers.*

Some children's ministries may allow children to play outside at this point. If yours does not, choose one of the following activities.

 ## Prayers Up, Blessings Down

Use one balloon per four to six children for this game. Explain that balloons represent our prayers as they go up to God, and His blessings as they come back down to us. The kids will lie down on their backs in a group, legs all pointed toward the center. Toss the balloons toward the center where the kids will use their feet to keep the balloons going up as they fall down. Move around the circle to push balloons back to the center as needed.

 ## Praise March

Choose familiar, exuberant praise music to play on a tape or CD. The class will march around the room singing and praising God, like the people of Judah did after God conquered their enemies.

 ## ON THE FAST TRACK! *(Take-Home Papers)*

(Optional) Treasure box: **Anyone want a prize from the treasure box?** Show the *On the Fast Track!* take-home papers. **Here's your *On the Fast Track!* paper to take home. You can do the activities and learn a Bible verse to earn a prize next week. Just have your parents or guardian sign the *Fast Track!* ticket and bring it back next week to get to choose something from the treasure box!**

Distribute the take-home papers just before children leave.

LESSON NINE: Giving Thanks for Creation

Memory Verse:
Be joyful always; pray continually; give thanks in all circumstances, for this is God's will for you in Christ Jesus (1 Thessalonians 5:16-18).
*Note: Early elementary verse in **bold** type.*

Bible Basis:
Genesis 1—2:1

Bible Truth:
We pray to thank God.

How do we pray?

You Will Need:

- [ ] 1 poster board
- [ ] red construction paper
- [ ] 7 paper bags
- [ ] piece of fruit (real or plastic)
- [ ] a small globe
- [ ] toy fish
- [ ] flashlight
- [ ] toy animal and realistic human doll
- [ ] blue inflated balloon
- [ ] jar of water
- [ ] large star of any material
- [ ] pillow
- [ ] treat jar
- [ ] *Use the Clues!* bag and previous objects
- [ ] *On the Fast Track! #9* take-home paper
- [ ] *StationMaster Card #9*
- [ ] *(Optional)* treasure box
- [ ] *(Optional)* Snack: plastic cups, spoons, prepared pudding, various mix-ins such as chocolate chips, dried fruit pieces, cookie crumbles, mini-marshmallows
- [ ] *(Optional)* Activity: large sheet of butcher paper, old magazines (one for each child)

When you see this icon, it means preparation will take more than five minutes.

GET SET!
(Lesson Preparation)

- ■ ⏱ Print today's Bible memory verse on a poster board:
  Be joyful always; pray continually; give thanks in all circumstances, for this is God's will for you in Christ Jesus (1 Thessalonians 5:16-18).
  Hang the poster board at the front of the classroom.
- ■ ⏱ Place a globe (green), flashlight (red), inflated balloon (blue), jar of water *and* a fruit (purple), star (yellow), fish (white), an animal *and* the human doll (brown), and pillow (pink) in individual bags and fold them closed. Color code each bag with marker or crayon based on the color in parentheses after each object.
- ■ Cut a large heart from the construction paper.
- ■ Make a copy of *On the Fast Track! #9* take-home paper for each child.
- ■ Make a copy of *StationMaster Card #9* for each helper.
- ■ Set out the treat jar, *Use the Clues!* bag, and (optional) treasure box.
- ■ Set up snack or outside play activities if you use these in your children's ministry

TICKETS PLEASE!
(Welcome and Bible Connection)

■ **Objective:** *To excite children's interest and connect their own experiences with the Bible Truth, children will create posters that reflect the beauty of creation.*

Welcome Time Activity: Poster Pinups

■ **Materials:** *large sheets of paper or whiteboard space, markers*
Set out large pieces of paper or clear space at the whiteboard. As children arrive, talk to them about the Garden of Eden and let them create pictures of what they think the garden might have looked like. Mount the posters on the wall if possible.

When everyone has arrived, welcome the children and offer them a treat from the treat jar. Say: **God likes it when children come and talk to Him. Whenever they do, He rewards them with His presence. These treats remind us how much He enjoys our time with Him.** Children may finish their treat now, or set it aside to take home later.

(Optional) If children returned a signed *Fast Track!* ticket, they may choose a prize from the treasure box also.

Sharing Time and Bible Connection

Introduce today's lesson by discussing the following questions with your students in the large group. As you talk, give every child the opportunity to say something.

■ **When was the last time you said "thank you" for something?**
■ **What's your favorite thing God created?**
■ **Why do you think we need to tell God thank you?** (He created so much for us to enjoy, He gave Jesus as a sacrifice for our sins)

Help connect the discussion to the Bible story children are about to hear from Genesis 1—2:1

Everything you enjoy today is from God—from the food you ate this morning, to the people in your family, and even the light that let you see what clothes to put on! Just think what a day would be like without your family, your friends, light to see by, yummy food, and beautiful things like flowers and wild animals. God made all of it for us to enjoy, and <u>He deserves our thanks. That's another reason we have to pray.</u> Let's see just what we have to thank God for.

ALL ABOARD FOR BIBLE TRUTH!

Genesis 1–2:1

(Bible Discover and Learn Time)

- ■ *Objective:* Children will study Genesis 1—2:1 and learn that we should thank God for the creation He made for our enjoyment.
- ■ *Materials:* 7 color-coded bags containing objects, Bible, construction paper heart

Show children the closed bags. Have them sit so they can pass the bags around as you tell the story. When you call for a color, the child holding that bag should come to the front, take out the object, and stand holding it during the rest of the story.

Raise your hand if God has given you something you're thankful for. Observe and affirm with a nod. **God has given us tons of wonderful things. He's done so much for us.**

Hand the bags out so children begin passing them around the group. Read from the Bible: **In the very beginning, God made the heavens and the earth. The earth was completely dark. Only God could live there. He walked over the surface of the deep.**

Then God said, "Let there be light." Call the child holding the red-coded bag and have the child remove the flashlight. Children should stop passing the bags. **Say with me, "Thank You, God, for giving us light."** Have children repeat this after you. **Then He divided the light from the darkness and made day and night.** Children may pass the bags again.

The second day God separated the waters above the earth from the waters below the earth. Call up the child with the blue-coded bag; have child remove balloon. **God put air between the water on the planet and above the earth. God named that the sky. And now there was air to breathe. Say with me, "Thank You, God, for separating the waters."** Children repeat line.

On day three, God pulled all the waters together and made oceans and lakes. Call on child with the purple bag to take out the water. **Now there was dry land. He called the land earth and the water areas, seas. God said it was good. Let's say, "Thank You, God, for making the earth and the seas."** Children repeat line. **But wait! God wasn't finished yet!** Now ask child to pull out fruit. **Next He made plants and fruit trees and all kinds of growing things.**

The earth is four days old now. On this day, God threw the sun, moon, and stars into the sky. Call up child with the yellow bag and have child remove the star. **This made day and night. At the same time, God created the seasons of summer, winter, fall, and spring. Say with me, "Thank You, God, for light to rule the day and the night."** Children repeat line.

God still had plenty to create. On day five He made all the fish and animals that live in the water. Call up the child with the white bag to show the fish. **God made birds to fly everywhere in the sky. He created the great sea monsters and everything that moves in the water or the air. Whew! Let's say, "Thank You, God, for all the animals in the water, and all the birds you made."** Children repeat line.

Now we're on the sixth day. Can you guess what God made next?

Accept ideas. Call up child with the brown bag. **God created giraffes and gerbils and skunks and bears—every kind of animal. And (dramatic pause) He made us! This was the day God made the first people. So let's say, "Thank You, God, for making animals and for making us."** Children repeat line.

Well, what's left? Call up child with the pink bag. **God liked what He made so much that He rested. He wants us to rest one day a week too. Let's say, "Thank You, God, for letting us have a fun day of rest."** Children repeat line.

There's one more thing to thank God for. Show children the red paper heart. **It's Jesus! We've sinned, and that means we're separated from God. To help us get back together with God again, Jesus died on the cross in our place. Jesus' love and what He did for us is a huge thing to be thankful for.**

Thank the "volunteers," have them set aside their objects and bags, and sit down.

Use the Clues!
(Bible Review)

Let's see what you remember about God's creation.

- **What was the first thing God made?** (heavens and the earth)
- **After He made everything, what did He do on day seven?** (rest)
- **Since God made all these things for us to enjoy, what should we do?** (thank Him)
- **What else could you thank God for?** (affirm other suggestions, then help kids focus on Jesus as the payment for our sin)
- **Why do <u>we thank God when we pray</u>?** (God has done so much for us, He deserves our thanks)

Anything you enjoy or do during the day is something you can thank God for. Your prayers can just be a short thank you for things you enjoy or have because God loves you. Take the paper heart from the bag. **This heart reminds us of Jesus' love that let Him die for us. As you pass it around, you can tell Jesus thank you for loving you that much.** After the heart has gone around the circle, put it in the *Use the Clues!* bag. **<u>Whenever you pray this week, remember to thank God for something</u>**.

Can you remember the other lessons we've learned about prayer? Bring out the *Use the Clues!* bag with objects from previous lessons. On page 84 you'll find the objects, story, and prayer truth they represent. Have volunteers pull an object from the bag and try to remember the story and prayer truth.

BIBLE MEMORY WAYPOINT!   1 Thessalonians 5:16-18
(Scripture Memory)

- ***Objective:*** *Children will hide God's Word in their hearts for guidance, protection, and encouragement.*

Read the memory verse from the poster. Point to each word as you read it:

Be joyful always; pray continually; give thanks in all circumstances, for this is God's will for you in Christ Jesus (1 Thessalonians 5:16-18).

To help children memorize the verse, divide them into four groups. Have them sit in a squared-off circle, one group per side.

The first group should stand and say, **"Be joyful always"** then sit down.
Quickly, the second group should stand to say, **"Pray continually,"** then sit again.
The third group stands and says, **"Give thanks in all circumstances"** then sits.
Finally group four stands and says, **"For this is God's will for you."**
All the groups stand to say, **"In Christ Jesus (1 Thessalonians 5:16-18)."**

Challenge the class to see how quickly they can do the verse without pauses. Repeat the verse in this way until it's familiar.

 ## PRAYER STATION

■ *Objective:* Children will explore and practice prayer for themselves.
■ *Materials:* copies of StationMaster Card #9 for each helper

Break into small groups of three to five children. Assign a teen or adult helper to each small group and give each helper a copy of StationMaster Card #9 (see Resources Section).

 ## SNACK STOP: CREATION PARFAITS (Optional)

If you plan to provide a snack, this is an ideal time to serve it.

■ *Materials:* plastic cups, spoons, prepared pudding, various mix-ins such as chocolate chips, dried fruit pieces, cookie crumbles, mini-marshmallows

Tell children just as God created the world and everything in it, they get to create their snack. Spoon a portion of pudding in each child's cup, then let them add toppings to their liking. As they create and eat, go around the table and ask each child to name something God made. See how long you can go without someone being speechless.

Note: Always be aware of children with food allergies and have another option on hand if necessary.

APPLICATION

■ **Objective:** *Children will have opportunities to show how the lesson works in their own lives through activities and take-home papers.*

Some children's ministries may allow children to play outside at this point. If yours does not, choose one of the following activities.

 ## Creation Scramble

Choose four aspects of creation. Whisper one of the four in each child's ear, so that there's an equal distribution of all four throughout the class. On your signal, the children scramble around the room saying their word and linking up with others of the same word until four groups have formed. Play again with different words. Make this more challenging by having more words per game. Examples of words: light, dark, water, sky, fish, animals, people, rest, heavens, earth, seas, plants, birds.

 ## Magazine Mural

Scatter magazines around the tables so children can tear or cut out pictures that show what God created in the creation week. They can include "resting" images to represent day seven. Have them glue their pictures onto a long strip of butcher paper in correct order to create a visual timeline of creation. Mount the mural on the wall.

 ### ON THE FAST TRACK! *(Take-Home Papers)*

(Optional) Treasure box: **Who can remind us how to earn a prize from the treasure box? Yes! By taking this** *On the Fast Track!* **paper home, doing the activities, and memorizing the Bible verse. When you bring back the** *Fast Track!* **ticket signed next week, you'll get to choose a prize from the treasure box!** Show students the ticket.

Distribute the take-home papers just before children leave.

LESSON TEN: Praising God

Memory Verse:
Let everything that has breath praise the LORD. Praise the LORD (Psalm 150:6).

Bible Truth:
We pray to praise God.

Bible Basis:
Genesis 1:1; Psalms 19:14; 91:2; 99:9; 111:4; 139:1, 7-8; Isaiah 9:6; John 1:29; 1 Timothy 1:17; 6:15; Hebrews 10:30; 1 John 4:14, 16; Revelation 11:16-17

How do we pray?

You Will Need:

- [ ] large plastic eggs, one per child + 1 more
- [ ] Characteristics of God pages 88-90 (see Resources)
- [ ] small wrapped candies
- [ ] white felt banner
- [ ] one half-inch wooden dowel, 36" long
- [ ] CD/tape player with praise music
- [ ] a thin dowel 18" long for each student
- [ ] 1 poster board
- [ ] assorted colors of construction paper
- [ ] butcher paper
- [ ] treat jar
- [ ] *Use the Clues!* bag and previous objects
- [ ] *On the Fast Track! #10* take-home paper
- [ ] *StationMaster Card #10*
- [ ] *(Optional)* treasure box
- [ ] *(Optional)* Snack: mini-cookies or fruit chunks, creamy fruit-flavored yogurt, small plastic cups or bowls
- [ ] *(Optional)* Activity: index cards, praise flag from Bible story, card stock

When you see this icon, it means preparation will take more than five minutes.

 GET SET!
(Lesson Preparation)

- Print today's Bible memory verse on a poster board:
  Let everything that has breath praise the LORD. Praise the LORD (Psalm 150:6).
  Hang the poster board at the front of the classroom.
- Copy Characteristics of God pages 88-90. Allow one square for each student (duplicate pictures if necessary). Cut the squares apart. Place one square inside each plastic egg with a piece of candy.
- Hide the plastic eggs around the classroom.
- Glue white felt to the dowel to make a flag; find a place to set this flag in your classroom.
- Make a copy of *On the Fast Track #10* take-home paper for each child.
- Make a copy of *StationMaster Card #10* for each helper.
- Set out treat jar, *Use the Clues!* bag and previous objects, and (optional) treasure box.
- Set up snack or outside play activities if you include these items in your children's ministry.
- Create a sample praise banner with construction paper and a dowel for the Welcome Time Activity. *Note: During Bible story time, you will also make a classroom praise flag out of felt.*
- Cue up the praise song in the CD/tape player.

Optional flag stand:
Fill an empty coffee can with sand or rocks, then stick the dowel in the can so it will stand up.

TICKETS PLEASE!
(Welcome and Bible Connection)

■ **Objective:** *To excite children's interest and connect their own life experiences with the Bible Truth, children will make a paper banner to praise God.*

Welcome Time Activity: Praise Banners

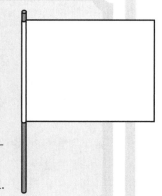

■ **Materials:** *construction paper, markers or crayons, tape, thin dowels, sample praise banner*

As children arrive, direct them to a table where you have set out the paper, tape, and dowels, plus your sample praise banner. Encourage children to create their own praise banner with their illustrations, words, and phrases—anything that honors God and can be used in a praise time. When the banner is finished, glue it to a dowel.

When everyone has arrived, call children to the lesson area and welcome them. Offer them a treat from the treat jar. Say: **God loves it when we praise Him. Today He's pleased you've come to learn about praising Him when you pray. Because praise is sweet to God, have a sweet treat before we begin.** Children may finish their treat now, or set it aside to take home later.

(Optional) If children returned a signed *Fast Track!* ticket, they may choose a prize from the treasure box also.

Sharing Time and Bible Connection

Introduce today's lesson by discussing the following questions with your students in the large group. As you talk, give every child the opportunity to say something.

■ **Do you know what a compliment is?** (telling someone something about them that you think is special or cool)
■ **What kinds of things do people compliment you about?** If children hesitate, give an example like "You're fun," "You're smart," "You're very patient."
■ **Have you ever thought of telling God what is special or good about Him? What do you say?**

After discussion time, help your students connect their discussion to the Bible lesson they are about to hear from various texts:

One important thing to do when we pray is to praise God. This is when we tell Him why He's special. It's not the same as thanking Him for what He does. We pray to praise God because we want to tell Him

we know He's awesome. It reminds us of who God is. Praising God should be a part of our prayers often. So how do we praise God, anyway? How does it work? That's what we're going to find out today.

ALL ABOARD FOR BIBLE TRUTH!
(Bible Discover and Learn Time)

Various Passages

■ *Objective: Children will study various verses to understand what it means to praise God.*
■ *Materials: felt praise flag, praise music, CD/tape player, filled plastic eggs, crayons or markers, glue sticks*

Play the praise tape softly as background music. **To start our lesson, we're going on a treasure hunt. You're going to hunt for plastic eggs, but you may find only one egg! If you find another one, keep it a secret. Bring your one egg back to your seat and wait until everyone has found an egg. And don't open it until I tell you to.**

Once everyone has an egg, the children may open them and look at the pictures and verses inside. Give them a couple of minutes to color the pictures on their square of paper. Then one by one have students read their Scripture verse and tell about the picture. Ask older children to partner with younger ones to help with reading.

Next, each child should glue their square (picture-side-up) to the white felt praise flag. Once glued, they should read their characteristic and Bible reference.

Look at all the great things there are that describe God! And these aren't even all of the things we know about God. Every paper we put up here tells us something about who God is. So each of these is something we can praise God for.

Our praise flag is cool! Have children make a circle. Turn up the praise music and lead the children in singing praises to God. Those who don't know the song can listen. **As we listen or sing, we'll pass our praise flag around the circle. This is one way to praise God.**

What other ways can we praise God? Affirm children's ideas of praise. <u>When we pray, we can praise God</u>.

Use the Clues!
(Bible Review)

Okay, let's see what other lessons you remember about **prayer.** Bring out the *Use the Clues!* bag with objects from previous lessons. On page 84 you'll find the objects, story, and prayer truth they represent. Have volunteers pull an object from the bag and try to remember the story and prayer truth.

- **What does it mean to praise God?** (we appreciate who God is with our words, prayer, our bodies, and our thoughts)
- **Why should <u>we praise God when we pray?</u>** (He deserves it, He enjoys it, it helps us know God better)
- **What are some things you can praise God for?** (children may name any of the characteristics from the Bible lesson)
- **How can you praise God this week?**

<u>Praise should be part of all our prayers</u>. Anytime we pray is a good chance to praise God for being loving, forgiving, patient, strong, or any other qualities we know about Him. God loves to hear our praise. Show an empty plastic egg. **This egg is our reminder that we can praise God.** Let children pass it around and name one thing they want to praise God for. Then put the egg back in the bag.

BIBLE MEMORY WAYPOINT!   Psalm 150:6
(Scripture Memory)

- **Objective:** *Children will hide God's Word in their hearts for guidance, protection, and encouragement.*

Read this week's memory verse from the poster. Point to each word as you read it:

Let everything that has breath praise the LORD. Praise the LORD (Psalm 150:6).

Put the words and reference to a simple tune you make up. Rehearse it with the children a few times, then let the children dance or use their bodies to express the words. Some children may choose not to do so, which is acceptable too.

PRAYER STATION

- **Objective:** *Children will explore and practice prayer for themselves in small groups.*
- **Materials:** *Copies of StationMaster Card #10 for each helper*

Break the large group into smaller groups of three to five children. Assign a teen or adult helper to each small group and give each helper a copy of *StationMaster Card #10* (see Resources Section) with ideas for group discussion and prayer.

SNACK STOP: PRAISE DIPPERS (Optional)

If you plan to provide a snack, this is an ideal time to serve it.

■ *Materials:* *cookies or fruit pieces (apple wedges, grapes), creamy fruit-flavored yogurt, small plastic cups or bowls*

Provide a small portion of fruity yogurt for each child and several mini-cookies or pieces of fruit. As they dip their cookies or fruit in the yogurt, have them praise God for something. Connect: Dipping their food is like adding praise to their prayers—it makes them even sweeter to God's ears.

Note: Always be aware of children with food allergies and have another option on hand if necessary.

APPLICATION

■ *Objective:* *Children will have opportunities to show how the lesson works in their own lives through activities and take-home papers.*

Some children's ministries may allow children to play outside at this point. If yours does not, choose one of the following activities.

Praise Relay

Divide into teams of six players each. Have each player write down (with help if needed) on an index card one of the characteristics of God from the Bible lesson. Use the praise flag for ideas. Each team needs six different characteristics. Place each team's cards at the far end of the room. Team members line up at the other end, opposite their set of cards. At GO!, the first player from each team races to their stack, reads the characteristic loudly, then races back to tag the next player, who does the same. Stand at the end with the cards to help younger children read the cards. Vary the game by having players walk backward, hop, skip, etc. to the cards. Change cards between teams also.

 Praise Bookmark

Provide card stock and markers for children to write down or draw some of the characteristics of God used during the Bible story. They can use the praise flag from the story time for ideas. Have them tell you where they'll keep their bookmark so it reminds them to praise God when they pray this week.

 ON THE FAST TRACK! *(Take-Home Papers)*

(Optional) Treasure box: **Here's your *On the Fast Track!* paper to take home. You can do the activities and learn a Bible verse to earn a prize next week. Just have your parents or another adult sign the *Fast Track!* ticket and bring it back next week to get to choose something from the treasure box!**

Distribute the take-home papers just before children leave.

LESSON ELEVEN: Forgiven!

Memory Verse:
For if you forgive men when they sin against you, your heavenly Father will also forgive you (Matthew 6:14).

Bible Basis:
John 8:1-11

Bible Truth:
We pray to confess and ask forgiveness.

How do we pray?

You Will Need:

- [ ] illustration of Jesus and the woman (Resources, 91)
- [ ] Bible time dress-up box
- [ ] baseball
- [ ] 1 poster board
- [ ] large bucket or empty trash basket
- [ ] small balls or paper wads
- [ ] treat jar
- [ ] *Use the Clues!* bag and previous objects
- [ ] *On the Fast Track #11* take-home paper
- [ ] *StationMaster Card #11*
- [ ] (Optional) treasure box
- [ ] (Optional) Snack: small plastic plates, prepared pudding, spoons, napkins or moist towelettes
- [ ] (Optional) Activity: newspaper, smooth stones, small brushes, acrylic paint

 When you see this icon, it means preparation will take more than five minutes.

 GET SET!
(Lesson Preparation)

- ■ 🕐 Print today's Bible memory verse on a poster board:
  For if you forgive men when they sin against you, your heavenly Father will also forgive you (Matthew 6:14).
  Hang the poster board on the wall at the front of the classroom.
- ■ Make a copy of *On the Fast Track #11* take-home paper for each child.
- ■ Make a copy of *StationMaster Card #11* for each helper.
- ■ Set out the treat jar, *Use the Clues!* bag, and (optional) treasure box.
- ■ Set up snack or outside play activities if you include these items in your children's ministry.
- ■ Make a copy of the illustration on page 91. Color it with markers.

TICKETS PLEASE!
(Welcome and Bible Connection)

- ■ *Objective: To excite children's interest and connect their own life experiences with the Bible Truth, children will play a game which involves throwing "stones."*

Welcome Time Activity: Rock Toss

■ *Materials: large bucket or empty trash can, small balls or paper wads*
Set a bucket or trash can six to ten feet from where children will line up. Players take turns trying to toss 2–3 balls or wads into the bucket. Tickle their curiosity by saying that today's lesson is about throwing stones.

When everyone has arrived, welcome children and offer them a treat from the treat jar. **God likes it when children come and learn about Him. Whenever they do, He rewards them with His presence. The treats remind us of that reward.** Children may finish their treat now, or set it aside to take home later.

(Optional) If children returned a signed *Fast Track!* ticket, they may choose a prize from the treasure box also.

Sharing Time and Bible Connection

To introduce today's lesson on prayer, ask for a volunteer and then hand that child a baseball. Ask the child to toss the ball up and catch it—very controlled and easy. **Imagine it's a sunny day and** (child) **is waiting outside for friends.** (child) **is throwing the ball up and catching it. Ahh, the sun feels great and you can't wait to see your friends.** (child) **throws the ball higher and higher—a little higher every time. Then a dog barks really loudly and the ball flies out of his hand. Oh no!** Pause dramatically. **Crash! The ball flies through the neighbor's window. How would** (child) **feel? What should** (child) **do?** Accept ideas. **Do you think** (child) **should tell the neighbors s/he's sorry and will get it fixed?** Thank volunteer, who can sit down.

■ **When was the last time you needed to say you were sorry to someone?**
■ **How do you feel when the person says, "That's okay. I forgive you?"** (thankful, happy, relieved)
■ **Are there times you should ask forgiveness, but you forget or don't want to? What keeps you from saying you're sorry when you've done wrong?** (fear, embarrassment, don't know what to say)

After discussion time, help your students connect their discussion to the Bible story they are about to hear from John 8. Show the illustration of Jesus and the woman.
Every one of us has done things wrong. That's right! And God knows all about it. We need to <u>say we're sorry and ask His forgiveness</u> when we've done wrong. Praying is how we do that. Saying we're sorry to God is called "confession." And even when it's hard and we're afraid or embarrassed, confessing and being forgiven takes it all away and makes you feel so much better. There's one lady in the Bible who found that out. Let's find out more about it.

📖 ALL ABOARD FOR BIBLE TRUTH!   John 8:1-11
(Bible Discover and Learn Time)

■ **Objective:** *Children will learn how Jesus forgave a woman her sins in John 8.*
■ **Materials:** *Bible time dress-up box, baseball,* Use the Clues! *bag*

Ask for several children to play the parts of the teachers and Pharisees. Ask another to be Jesus and one more to be the woman. Have volunteers choose something in the Bible time dress-up box. Cluster the Pharisees in one spot, with Jesus and the woman standing nearby, but apart.

Let me introduce today's characters. Indicate each as you introduce them. **Here we have the teachers of the law and the Pharisees. This is Jesus, and this is the woman who's the main character in the Bible story.**

The woman you see here was someone who lived in Jesus' time. She probably had the same kind of feelings as you would have if you'd broken someone's window with the baseball. She had done wrong and needed to be forgiven. How do you think her face would look? Let children show you, and have woman look humiliated and sad.

She felt even worse when the Jewish teachers of the law and the Pharisees brought her to Jesus to be punished. Have Pharisees look angry. **They weren't kind at all. In fact, they told Jesus, "According to our law, a woman caught doing this bad thing should be stoned." Stoned! The sad woman felt even worse. They wanted to throw rocks at her until she died. What a terrible punishment for her sin!**

The Pharisees were sure Jesus would have to do something about this woman. They waited to hear what He would say; but Jesus didn't say anything. Instead, He did something very surprising. He bent down and started to write words in the dirt with His finger. "Jesus" actor should do this. **How strange. Even the woman wondered what Jesus was doing. So the Pharisees kept asking Him what He would do.**

Finally, Jesus stood up. He looked right at those Pharisees and said, "If any one of you is perfect—if you have never done anything wrong yourself—you can throw the first rock." Then He bent down again and wrote in the dirt with His finger.

The teachers and the Pharisees were totally quiet. Every one of them knew they had done many wrong things. Who could throw the first rock at this sinful

woman? No one! They weren't any better than her! "Pharisees" should look down, embarrassed; "woman" should look surprised. **One by one, the teachers and Pharisees silently walked away.** Have them do so. **The woman wondered what Jesus would do to her. After all, she was guilty of doing wrong.**

Long pause. **Jesus stood up again. He looked around. "Where are the people who wanted to stone you?" He said to the woman. "Didn't anyone want to throw the first rock?"**

She shook her head. "No, sir."

"I won't throw one either. Go home, and don't do wrong anymore." Incredible! How do you think this woman felt now?

Let children respond. **She knew she'd done wrong. She thought she was going to die. Then all of a sudden Jesus told her that she was free!**

Have you ever felt like the woman in the Bible? Have children share about a time they were forgiven and how that felt. **When you know you did something wrong and deserve to be punished, then you also know how wonderful it feels to be forgiven. That's exactly what Jesus does for us when we ask Him. He cleans away the sin and leaves us free.**

Sometimes we still have to work out the consequences of our behavior. Remember the baseball example? If (child) **did really break the window, asking forgiveness is the first step. Then replacing the window is the right thing to do.**

Thank volunteers and have them return dress-up clothing and sit down.

Use the Clues!
(Bible Review)

Okay, let's see what you remember about this story.

- **Why did the teachers and Pharisees bring the woman to Jesus?** (she had done wrong—sinned—and they wanted her to be punished)
- **What did Jesus say to the teachers and Pharisees?** (whoever hasn't sinned can throw the first stone at the woman)
- **Why didn't any of the Pharisees throw a rock at the woman?** (all of them were just as guilty of sin as she was)
- **What did Jesus do about the woman?** (He forgave her)
- **How are you and I like that woman?** (we need Jesus' forgiveness for our sins)
- **How can we have our sins forgiven?** (by praying and confessing our sin and asking God to forgive us)

Every one of us needs forgiveness just like that woman. We are so blessed that Jesus will forgive us just as He did her. We can pray at any time to confess something we've done. We should do it often! Hold up the baseball. **This baseball can be our reminder than when we do wrong, we can pray and confess it. God will always hear us and forgive us.** Toss the ball to someone in the group. **When the ball comes to you, say, "I can ask God to forgive me when I sin."** Then toss the ball to someone else. After each child has participated, put the ball in the bag.

Now let's see what you remember about prayer from other lessons. Bring out the *Use the Clues!* bag. On page 84 you'll find the objects, story, and prayer truth they represent. Have volunteers pull an object from the bag and try to remember the story and prayer truth.

BIBLE MEMORY WAYPOINT!   Matthew 6:14
(Scripture Memory)

■ *Objective: Children will hide God's Word in their hearts for guidance, protection, and encouragement.*

Read this week's memory verse from the poster. Point to each word as you read it:

For if you forgive men when they sin against you, your heavenly Father will also forgive you (Matthew 6:14).

To help children memorize the verse, teach them some actions to go with it:

For if you forgive men *(shake hands with others around you)*
when they sin against you, *(slap your own hand)*
your heavenly Father *(put your arms above your head)*
will also forgive you. *(cross your arms over your chest)*
Matthew 6:14 *(stomp with each syllable)*

Repeat the verse and actions until the children become familiar with the words.

PRAYER STATION

■ *Objective: Children will explore and practice prayer for themselves in small groups.*
■ *Materials: Copies of* StationMaster Card #11 *for each helper (see Resources)*

Break into small groups of three to five children. Assign a teen or adult helper to each small group and give each helper a copy of *StationMaster Card #11*.

SNACK STOP: FINGER PAINTING (Optional)

If you plan to provide a snack, this is an ideal time to serve it.

■ *Materials: small plastic plates, prepared pudding, spoons, napkins or moist towelettes*

Spoon some pudding onto each child's plate and let them all finger paint in the pudding, as Jesus wrote in the dirt. After writing words such as confess, sin, forgive, and free, they can eat their finger paint!

Note: Always be aware of children with food allergies and have another option on hand if necessary.

APPLICATION

■ **Objective:** *Children will have opportunities to show how the lesson works in their own lives through activities and take-home papers.*

Some children's ministries may allow children to play outside at this point. If yours does not, choose one of the following activities.

 Forgiven Tag

Designate one player as "it," and define game boundaries. When tagged by "it," players must squat until another player touches them and says, "You're forgiven." Then the tagged player may rejoin the game. Add more challenge by adding more "it" taggers.

 Rock Painting

Lay newspaper on tables. Provide some smooth stones, small brushes, and acrylic paint. Have children paint stones with symbols, words, or drawings that relate to today's Bible story and theme of confession and forgiveness. After children are finished, have them show others their stone creation and tell what their symbols and art mean.

 ON THE FAST TRACK! *(Take-Home Papers)*

(Optional) Treasure box: **Here's your *On the Fast Track!* paper to take home. You can do the activities and learn a Bible verse to earn a prize next week. Just have your parents or another adult sign the *Fast Track!* ticket and bring it back next week to get to choose something from the treasure box!**

Distribute the take-home papers just before children leave.

Memory Verse:

Be still, and know that I am God; I will be exalted among the nations, I will be exalted in the earth (Psalm 46:10).
*Note: Early elementary verse in **bold** type.*

Bible Basis:
1 Samuel 3:1-21

Bible Truth:
When we pray, we should listen to God.

How do we pray?

You Will Need:

- [ ] Bible time dress-up box
- [ ] 2 poster boards
- [ ] CD/tape player
- [ ] music CD/tape
- [ ] play dough
- [ ] picture of ear (Resources, 84)
- [ ] plate of small cookies, such as animal crackers
- [ ] *Use the Clues!* bag
- [ ] *On the Fast Track #12* take-home paper
- [ ] *StationMaster Card #12*
- [ ] (Optional) treasure box
- [ ] (Optional) Snack: small paper cups, finger foods (raisins, round chocolate candies, graham cracker creatures, fish crackers, etc.), CD/tape player, CD or tape
- [ ] (Optional) Activity: blindfold, obstacle course, kite string, 2 styrofoam cups per child

When you see this icon, it means preparation will take more than five minutes.

 GET SET!
(Lesson Preparation)

- ▪ 🌐 Print today's Bible memory verse twice, on *two* poster boards:
  Be still, and know that I am God; I will be exalted among the nations, I will be exalted in the earth (Psalm 46:10).
  Hang one poster board at the front of the classroom. Cut up the other into large puzzle pieces.
- ▪ Set up the CD or tape player and music, set to high volume.
- ▪ Put the cookies on a plate.
- ▪ Make a copy of *On the Fast Track #12* take-home paper for each child.
- ▪ Make a copy of *StationMaster Card #12* for each helper.
- ▪ Set out *Use the Clues!* bag and previous objects, and *(optional)* treasure box.
- ▪ Set up snack or outside play activities if you include these items in your children's ministry.

 TICKETS PLEASE!
(Welcome and Bible Connection)

- ▪ **Objective:** *To excite children's interest and connect their own life experiences with the Bible Truth, children create play dough figures that emphasize listening.*

Welcome Time Activity: Play Dough Play

■ *Materials:* play dough (see recipe for play dough in Lesson 4)
As children arrive, let them model from play dough something that has large ears. Have children guess what others have made.

When everyone has arrived and play dough figures have been set aside, turn on the praise music and begin to play it very loudly in the room. Welcome each child in a very quiet voice, gesture them to move to the lesson area, and invite them to help themselves to a cookie from the plate. *Be sure that the music is so loud the children cannot hear your voice.*

(*Optional*) If children returned a signed *Fast Track!* ticket, they may choose a prize from the treasure box also.

Sharing Time and Bible Connection

When everyone is seated, turn off the music and ask:

■ **Did you enjoy the cookies I said you could have?** (Children will protest that they didn't hear you.)
■ **Why couldn't you hear me?**
■ **Why is it important to be a good listener and not let noise get in the way?** (if you don't, you might miss important information)
■ **What are some times or places it is *especially* important to listen carefully?** (school, parents, doctors, police or firefighters giving instructions)

Yes, those are important times to listen. But it is most important that we listen to God. Today's Bible story from the Old Testament is about a young boy named Samuel who listened to God.

ALL ABOARD FOR BIBLE TRUTH!   1 Samuel 3:1-21
(Bible Discover and Learn Time)

■ *Objective: Children will study 1 Samuel 3 and hear that a young person was called to ministry and how important it is to listen to God.*
■ *Materials: Use the Clues! bag, picture of an ear (see Resources, 84)*

Instruct the students to lie down on the floor and pretend to sleep while you tell the story. Tell them to listen carefully. **When I get to the parts where Samuel says, "Here I am!" you should jump up and say, "Here I am!"**

When Samuel was just about your age, he lived at the tabernacle. That was the tent of worship where the people of Israel brought their offerings to God. He did all kinds of things to help out around the tabernacle. Samuel served God by helping a priest named Eli. **What is a priest?** Listen to responses, then explain that a priest is a leader in the church.

Back in those days, God didn't speak to His people very often. And even though Samuel served at the tabernacle, he didn't know God. He was learning about God, of course, but didn't know Him yet.

One night while Samuel was sleeping, he heard a voice call his name. "Samuel" (say this softly). **He woke right up! Of course Samuel thought it was Eli. Who else would call him in the middle of the night? Samuel quickly jumped out of bed. He ran to Eli and said, "Here I am. You called me?"** Wait for children to jump up and say, "Here I am!" Then tell them to go back to sleep. **But Eli just yawned and said, "Samuel, my boy, I didn't call you. Go back to sleep."**

So Samuel went back to bed. He lay there wide awake. Suddenly, he heard the voice again: "Samuel" (say this more firmly). **Samuel got up again and ran back to Eli. He didn't want to miss what Eli had to tell him. "Here I am!" he said.** Wait for children to jump up as before. **But Eli said, "I didn't really call you, Samuel. Go back to bed."**

Samuel was confused. He went back to his bed, but he couldn't sleep at all! Then he heard the voice speak a third time: "Samuel!" (say this sharply). **Again he ran to Eli and said, "Here I am!"** Wait for children to jump up. **This time Eli just looked at him. He was thinking hard. Finally he said, "Samuel, I understand now. The voice you hear is the Lord calling you. The next time the Lord speaks, tell Him you're listening."**

Samuel ran back to his bed and lay there quietly. He really wanted to hear what the Lord had to say. Then he heard the voice: "Samuel. Samuel." Samuel answered, "Speak, Lord. I am Your servant, and I am listening."

Well, God spoke and what He had to say made Samuel's ears tingle! God gave Samuel a warning that He was going to punish Eli's family. Eli's sons were priests too, but they kept sinning against God. And Eli did not stop them. They were hurting God's people by being bad leaders.

Samuel listened carefully that night and for all the rest of his life. God spoke often to him and gave him messages for the people of Israel. Like Samuel, <u>we should listen to God</u>.

God talks to us, but not always in lots of words like we use. He sure does want us to <u>listen when we pray</u>, and not just talk. Sometimes listening to God means being still and waiting. It means always having your ears and mind ready to hear Him.

Use the Clues!
(Bible Review)

Okay, let's see what you remember from other lessons about prayer. Bring out the *Use the Clues!* bag with objects from previous lessons. On page 84 you'll find the objects, story, and prayer truth they represent. Have volunteers pull an object from the bag and try to remember the story and prayer truth.

- ■ **How did God speak to Samuel?** (with a voice in the night)
- ■ **What did Eli tell Samuel to say?** ("Speak Lord; I'm listening.")
- ■ **How might God speak to us today?**

(when we're reading the Bible or hearing it, through other people who love God, in your heart you will have peace)

Samuel listened carefully because he wanted to follow God's direction. When Samuel grew up, God made him an important leader. He could trust Samuel to listen and obey Him. Did you know that we can listen when we pray? We usually think of praying as talking to God. Show children the picture of the ear. **This picture of an ear reminds us that <u>when we pray, we should listen to God</u> the way Samuel did.** Pass around the picture of the ear, and have each child say, "We should listen to God." Put the picture in the *Use the Clues!* bag.

BIBLE MEMORY WAYPOINT!
(Scripture Memory)

Psalm 46:10

- ■ *Objective: Children will hide God's Word in their hearts for guidance, protection, and encouragement.*

Read the memory verse from the poster. Point to each word as you read it:

Be still, and know that I am God; I will be exalted among the nations, I will be exalted in the earth (Psalm 46:10).

To help children memorize the Bible verse, they can assemble a puzzle of the verse. Scramble the pieces and hand them out randomly to children of various ages. Let them work together to put the puzzle together, then have everyone read the verse together. Undo the puzzle and have other children try it. See if they can be more speedy than the first group. Say: **Listen,** then have a confident reader read the assembled verse.

PRAYER STATION

- **Objective:** *Children will explore and practice prayer for themselves in small groups.*
- **Materials:** *Copies of* StationMaster Card #12 *for each helper*

Break into small groups of three to five children. Assign a teen or adult helper to each small group and give each helper a copy of *StationMaster Card #12* (see Resources).

SNACK STOP: HEAR IT, EAT IT (Optional)

If you plan to provide a snack, this is an ideal time to serve it.

- **Materials:** *small paper cups, finger food of choice (raisins, round chocolate candies, graham cracker creatures, fish crackers, etc.), CD/tape player, CD or tape*

Choose a song with some words that repeat. Choose one or two words and tell the children to listen for those words. When they hear one of those words, they can eat a bite of their snack.

Note: Always be aware of children with food allergies and have another option on hand if necessary.

APPLICATION

- **Objective:** *Children will have opportunities to show how the lesson works in their own lives through activities and take-home papers.*

Some children's ministries may allow children to play outside at this point. If yours does not, choose one of the following activities.

Obstacle Course

Set up an obstacle course, and use the children as some of the "obstacles." For example, two students can hold a jump rope and wiggle it on the floor; others can hold up a hula hoop for children to climb through; several can wave their arms to create a passageway for a player to travel through. Use other items in the room also—tables to crawl under, chairs to circle, a book to jump over.

To play, a child is blindfolded and must listen to you give directions from the other end of the obstacle course while the other kids sing, play musical instruments, laugh, and make noise. Then, allow child to repeat the course with the room quiet, listening to your voice. Young children may need an older guide to help navigate the course.

 Can You Hear Me Now?

Have children make simple telephones by piercing a hole in the bottom of two styrofoam cups. Push each end of a length of kite string into the two holes; knot inside. Kids can pair up to talk to each other on their "telephones." Before finishing the activity, remind children that just as friends talked to each other, God wants to talk to us when we pray.

 ON THE FAST TRACK! *(Take-Home Papers)*

(Optional) Treasure box: **Here's your *On the Fast Track!* paper to take home. You can do the activities and learn a Bible verse to earn a prize next week. Just have your parents or another adult sign the *Fast Track!* ticket and bring it back next week to get to choose something from the treasure box!**

Distribute the take-home papers just before children leave.

LESSON THIRTEEN: Our Ever-Ready God

When do we pray?

Memory Verse:

O LORD, you have searched me and you know me. You know when I sit and when I rise; you perceive my thoughts from afar (Psalm 139:1-2). ***Note:*** *Early elementary verse in* ***bold*** *type.*

Bible Basis:

Psalms 5:3; 55:17; 119:147; Matthew 14:13-21; Mark 1:35; Luke 6:12; Acts 22:6-11

Bible Truth:

We pray, knowing God will hear us anytime.

You Will Need:

- ☐ Bible time dress-up box
- ☐ 1 poster board
- ☐ colored pencils or fine-point markers
- ☐ a clock
- ☐ white removable labels (round, rectangular, or square)
- ☐ treat jar
- ☐ *Use the Clues!* bag
- ☐ *On the Fast Track #13* take-home paper
- ☐ *StationMaster Card #13*
- ☐ (Optional) treasure box
- ☐ (Optional) Snack: halved mini-bagels, spreadable cream cheese, raisins, pretzel sticks (2 per child), plastic knives
- ☐ (Optional) Activity: *Use the Clues!* bag, small prizes (optional)

When you see this icon, it means preparation will take more than five minutes.

 GET SET!

(Lesson Preparation)

- ■ 🌐 Print today's Bible memory verse on a poster board: **O LORD, you have searched me and you know me. You know when I sit and when I rise; you perceive my thoughts from afar (Psalm 139:1-2).** Hang the poster board at the front of the classroom.
- ■ Print the following on three separate papers: Morning; Noon and Afternoon; Evening and Night. Draw a sun on the Morning and the Noon and Afternoon sheets and a moon on the Evening and Night sheet.
- ■ 🌐 Use masking tape to make a circle on the floor. Make it large enough to hold all the children, and divide it into three equal sections. Tape one of the time-of-day signs in each segment of the circle.
- ■ Bookmark these passages in your Bible: Psalms 5:3; 55:17; 119:147; Matthew 14:13-21; Mark 1:35; Luke 6:12; Acts 22:6-11.
- ■ Make a copy of *On the Fast Track #13* take-home paper for each child.
- ■ Make a copy of *StationMaster Card #13* for each helper.
- ■ Set out treat jar, *Use the Clues!* bag and previous objects, and (optional) treasure box.
- ■ Set up snack or outside play activities if you include these items in your children's ministry.

TICKETS PLEASE!
(Welcome and Bible Connection)

■ **Objective:** *To excite children's interest and connect their own life experiences with the Bible Truth, children will make stickers that remind them to talk to God.*

Welcome Time Activity: Personalized Stickers

■ **Materials:** *white removable labels with paper backing (round, square, or rectangular), colored pencils or fine-point markers*

As children arrive, give them several white labels to create a set of personal stickers that will remind them to talk to God. They can draw or write words on the stickers (praying hands, cross, praise words, etc.). Challenge children to use the stickers at home or school to remind them to pray.

When everyone has arrived, call children to the lesson area and welcome them. Offer them a treat from the treat jar. Say: **No matter what time of day it is when you talk to God, He's so glad when you pray. Take a candy this morning for coming to learn about talking to God.** Children may finish their treat now, or set it aside to take home later.

(Optional) If children returned a signed *Fast Track!* ticket, they may choose a prize from the treasure box also.

Sharing Time and Bible Connection

Introduce today's lesson by discussing the following questions with your students in the large group. As you talk, give every child the opportunity to say something.

■ **What kinds of things do you do in the morning? The middle of the day? When it's dark?**
■ **Think about the last time you prayed to God. What part of the day was it?**
■ **Have you ever wondered if God is always awake or able to hear no matter what time it is when you pray?**

After discussion time, help your students connect their discussion to the Bible story they are about to hear from various Scripture passages:

No matter what time of the day or night you pray, God is ready to listen. He's not going to be busy eating dinner or sleeping or doing something else. There is not one single time of the day you can talk to God and He'll be too busy or tired to hear you. Wow! No one else can say that, can they? Let's see what God tells us about praying at different times.

ALL ABOARD FOR BIBLE TRUTH!
(Bible Discover and Learn Time)   **Various Passages**

■ *Objective: Children will study various Scripture passages and discover that God is always ready to listen to their prayers.*
■ *Materials: bookmarked Bible*

Today all of you are going to be part of the Bible story. Point to taped circle on the floor. **This circle is like a whole day. It is divided into morning, noon and afternoon, and evening and night.** Point to signs as you mention times. **Tell me something you would do in the morning.** Point to the "morning" segment and call on a couple of volunteers. Ask the same about the "noon and afternoon" and "evening and night" segments.

Great! Here's how you can be part of the story. I'm going to read some different verses about when God wants us to pray to Him. When you know which time that is, go stand in that section of the circle.

Read each passage. They can be read in any order. Praise those who stand in the correct section. Children should stand in the following sections of the circle for each passage:

■ Luke 6:12 (evening/night)
■ Mark 1:35 (morning)
■ Matthew 14:13-21 (evening/night)
■ Psalm 5:3 (morning)
■ Psalm 55:17 (morning, noon/afternoon, and evening/night)
■ Psalm 119:147 (morning)
■ Acts 22:6-11 (noon/afternoon)

Does the Bible say that there's only one good time to talk to God? (no) **In both the Old and New Testaments, God shows us that <u>we should pray to Him anytime we need to or want to</u>. Anytime you talk to God you're praying.**

Have children stand around the outside of the circle. **Now you can choose a time of day when you want to talk to God.** After children are settled, ask: **Since you chose that time, is that the only time God will be listening for you? No! He's always listening and welcomes our prayers every minute. Let's remember that <u>we can talk to God any time of day</u>.**

Use the Clues!
(Bible Review)

Close the lesson time with this discussion:

- **Name one time of day Jesus prayed.** (morning, afternoon, evening, night)
- **Does God hear our prayers for help when it's dark?** (yes)
- **What time does God want us to pray?** (anytime)

If we were going to put something in the *Use the Clues!* **bag to remind us about what** we've learned today, what kind of thing do you think we could use? Let children offer their suggestions. **Yes, a clock is a good reminder of what we learned today:** <u>God will hear us anytime</u>.

(Optional) If you choose to do the Use the Clues! *activity at the end of this lesson, omit it now:*

Okay, let's see what else you remember about talking to God in prayer. Bring out the *Use the Clues!* bag with objects from previous lessons. On page 84 you'll find the objects, story, and prayer truth they represent. Have volunteers pull an object from the bag and try to remember the story and prayer truth.

BIBLE MEMORY WAYPOINT!   Psalm 139:1-2
(Scripture Memory)

- **Objective:** *Children will hide God's Word in their hearts for guidance, protection, and encouragement.*

Read this week's memory verse from the poster. Point to each word as you read it:

O LORD, you have searched me and you know me. You know when I sit and when I rise; you perceive my thoughts from afar (Psalm 139:1-2).

To help children memorize the Bible verse, divide them into four groups. Have the groups stand in one large circle so they can see each other. Explain that they're going to echo parts of the verse. You'll point to the group who should echo, and they'll be a little quieter than the group before them.

Start by pointing to the first group and have them read the first phrase in a normal voice. Point to the next group to echo the same phrase but at a lower volume. Continue in the same way with all phrases through the other groups. Continue until the verse becomes familiar.

O LORD, you have searched me (echo)
and you know me. (echo)
You know when I sit and when I rise; (echo)
you perceive my thoughts from afar. (echo)
(Psalm 139:1-2) (echo)

PRAYER STATION

■ *Objective: Children will explore and practice prayer for themselves in large group.*

Children will pray in a large group today, but ask helpers to sit with small groups of children. You'll lead the group as a whole, using the *StationMaster* model in the Resources section, page 98. Helpers can assist younger children who are sitting near them to do what you suggest.

SNACK STOP: BAGEL CLOCKS (Optional)

If you plan to provide a snack, this is an ideal time to serve it.

■ *Materials: halved mini-bagels, spreadable cream cheese, raisins, pretzel sticks (2 per child), plastic knives*

Let's make edible clocks! Have children spread cream cheese on a mini-bagel half, then put 12 raisins around the outer edge. Use two pretzel sticks as clock hands. Have children show a time on their bagel clock when they want to remember to pray this week. Help younger children who aren't as familiar with clocks to put their pretzel sticks in the time position they choose.

Note: Always be aware of children with food allergies and have another option on hand if necessary.

APPLICATION

■ *Objective: Children will have opportunities to show how the lesson works in their own lives through activities and take-home papers.*

Some children's ministries may allow children to play outside at this point. If yours does not, choose one of the following activities.

Use the Clues! Review

Have one child at a time put a hand in the *Use the Clues!* bag and pull out an object. See if they can tell what truth about prayer the object represents and what Bible story or passages went with it. See page 84 for the list of objects and Bible passages.

If desired, you can hand out small prizes for getting the information correct. To spread out the prizes more, have one child name the Bible story, and a different child tell what truth the object demonstrates.

What Time Is It?

Let volunteers act out something they do during a specific time of day. Have them whisper the time of day to you before they start. Other players should guess what the actor is doing and what is its usual time of day.

ON THE FAST TRACK! *(Take-Home Papers)*

*This is the final lesson in the **Talking with God** series. If you will continue on with your students in the weeks that follow, remind them of the option below:*

(Optional) Treasure box: **Here's your *On the Fast Track!* paper to take home. You can do the activities and learn a Bible verse to earn a prize next week. Just have your parents or another adult sign the *Fast Track!* ticket and bring it back next week to get to choose something from the treasure box!**

If this is your final week with these students, encourage them to memorize their Scripture verse, complete the activities on their take-home papers, but most of all to be faithful in practicing what they've learned about prayer. God delights in talking with His children!

Distribute the take-home papers just before children leave.

USE THE CLUES!

Hold up the *Use the clues!* bag. Take out the yellow ball from Lesson 1 and ask, **What story does this ball remind us of? What do you remember about prayer from that lesson?** Allow children time to answer, and then have them say with you, **"We depend on God."** In the same way, remove each item in turn and challenge children to tell you the story and prayer truth associated with each one.

Object	Title	Prayer Truth
1. yellow ball	The Day the Sun Stood Still	We depend on God.
2. lamb	A Shepherd Sings Prayers to God	Prayer makes God happy.
3. photograph	Queen Esther Saves the Jews	God lets me be a part of His plan.
4. sugar cubes	The Talking Donkey	We obey God when we pray.
5. telephone	Jesus Talks and Listens to God	Prayer is conversation with God.
6. rocks	Showdown on Mount Carmel	We pray to know God's will.
7. empty medicine bottle	Great Faith Heals a Servant	We pray with faith.
8. musical instrument	God Wins a Big Battle	We can ask God for what we need.
9. heart	Giving Thanks for Creation	We can thank God.
10. plastic egg	Praising God	We can praise God.
11. baseball	Forgiven!	We should ask God for forgiveness.
12. picture of the ear	Stop and Listen to God	We should listen to God.
13. clock	Our Ever-Ready God	God will hear us anytime.

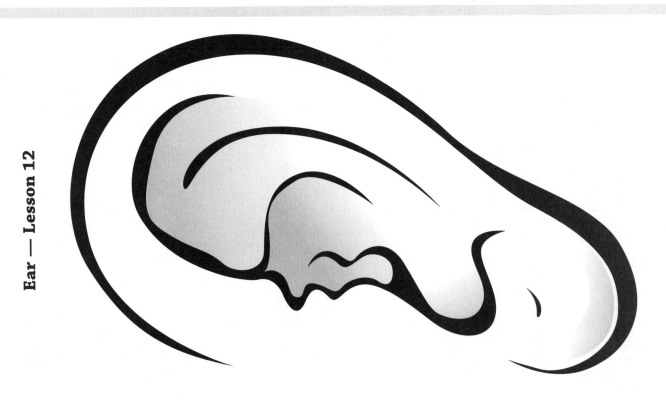

Ear — Lesson 12

Sick Servant — Lesson 7

Balaam — Lesson 4

Messengers — Lesson 4

Donkey — Lesson 4

Angel — Lesson 4

Mighty God

For to us a child is born, to us a son is given, and the government will be on his shoulders. And he will be called Wonderful Counselor, Mighty God, Everlasting Father, Prince of Peace (Isaiah 9:6).

Everlasting Father

For to us a child is born, to us a son is given, and the government will be on his shoulders. And he will be called Wonderful Counselor, Mighty God, Everlasting Father, Prince of Peace (Isaiah 9:6).

Prince of Peace

For to us a child is born, to us a son is given, and the government will be on his shoulders. And he will be called Wonderful Counselor, Mighty God, Everlasting Father, Prince of Peace (Isaiah 9:6).

Lamb of God

The next day John saw Jesus coming toward him and said, "Look, the Lamb of God, who takes away the sin of the world!" (John 1:29).

Judge

The Lord will judge his people (Hebrews 10:30).

Love

And so we know and rely on the love God has for us. God is love. Whoever lives in love lives in God, and God in him (1 John 4:16).

Characteristics of God — Lesson 10

Savior

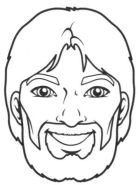

And we have seen and testify that the Father has sent his Son to be the Savior of the world (1 John 4:14).

God Almighty

We give thanks to you, Lord God Almighty, the One who is and who was (Revelation 11:17).

Rock

May the words of my mouth and the meditation of my heart be pleasing in your sight, O LORD, my Rock and my Redeemer (Psalm 19:14).

Redeemer

May the words of my mouth and the meditation of my heart be pleasing in your sight, O LORD, my Rock and my Redeemer (Psalm 19:14).

Fortress

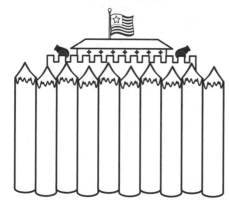

I will say of the LORD, "He is my refuge and my fortress, my God, in whom I trust" (Psalm 91:2).

Ever-Present

Where can I go from your Spirit? Where can I flee from your presence? If I go up to the heavens, you are there; if I make my bed in the depths, you are there (Psalm 139:7-8).

Characteristics of God — Lesson 10

Compassionate

He has caused his wonders to be remembered; the LORD is gracious and compassionate (Psalm 111:4).

Holy

Exalt the LORD our God and worship at his holy mountain, for the LORD our God is holy (Psalm 99:9).

Creator

In the beginning God created the heavens and the earth (Genesis 1:1).

All-Knowing

LORD, you have searched me and you know me (Psalm 139:1).

King of Kings

God, the blessed and only Ruler, the King of kings and Lord of lords (1 Timothy 6:15).

Immortal

Now to the King eternal, immortal, invisible, the only God, be honor and glory for ever and ever (1 Timothy 1:17).

Characteristics of God — Lesson 10

Jesus Forgiving the Woman — Lesson 11

Dear Parents,

During the next thirteen weeks in children's ministry, your child will learn about prayer. Our *Talking with God* curriculum explains the concepts of prayer in an exciting and interactive way and gives children an opportunity to build lifetime habits of prayer. Your child will explore why and how people pray and will learn to pray in small groups.

Talking with God uses the **imPACT** model of prayer to help children understand the four important activities of prayer—praise, ask, confess, and give thanks. Here are some discussion questions you may use at home to reinforce your child's growing desire to talk with God:

■ *Praise.* Ask your child: **What do you really like about God?** Listen to the responses. Then say: **Let's tell God we like these things about Him.** Encourage your child to tell God directly what he or she likes about Him.

■ *Ask.* It is important for children to know that God cares about their needs. We can ask God to help us, our families, and our friends with any problems. He wants everyone to ask Him for what they need. Ask: **What would you like to ask God?** Let your child name some prayer requests. Then say: **Let's tell God about these needs.** Take turns praying for these needs.

■ *Confess.* Tell your child that we all do things we wish we didn't do. Sometimes our actions or words hurt someone and then we are sorry. Ask: **What's one thing that you wish you didn't do this last week?** Listen to the response. Then say: **Let's confess our sin to God and tell Him we're sorry.** Together, bow heads and confess this sin before God.

■ *Give thanks.* Ask: **What are some things that you're thankful that God has done for you or has given to you?** Listen to the responses. Then say: **Let's tell God thank you for these things.** Take turns thanking God.

Since prayer is such an important concept, your child will receive a take-home paper for each lesson, designed to support the Bible Truth for that day. These take-home papers will include fun activities, a Bible memory verse, and a prayer challenge. Some of the activities invite the involvement of the whole family. Encourage your child to complete these activities and bring the signed *Fast Track!* ticket the following Sunday.

If you have any questions about this study, please feel free to discuss them with the children's ministry leaders. We are excited about what God is going to do in the lives of our children. We would appreciate your prayers for the teachers and children.

In His Name,

Children's Ministry Coordinator

Dear Children's Ministry Helper,

Welcome to *Discipleship Junction*! During the next 13 weeks, you will play a major role in the lives of children as you teach them about prayer, and pray with them in small groups. The *Talking with God* curriculum will help you build habits of prayer into their lives that will last a lifetime.

The **imPACT** model of prayer will remind children about the four important activities of prayer: praise, ask, confess, and give thanks:

■ *Praise. Ask:* **What do you really like about God?** Let volunteers briefly respond, then say: Let's tell God we like these things about Him. Help children talk to God directly.

■ *Ask.* Ask children: **What would you like to ask God?** Allow children to give prayer requests, then say: **Let's tell God about these needs.** It is important for children to know that God cares about everyone's needs. Have them take turns praying for the needs in their lives.

■ *Confess.* We all do things we wish we didn't do. Sometimes our actions or words hurt someone and then we are sorry. Ask them: **What's one thing that you wish you didn't do this last week?** Give children time to answer, then say: **Let's confess our sins to God and tell Him we're sorry.**

■ *Give thanks.* When giving thanks, ask your group: **Tell one thing that you're thankful that God has done for you.** Let children share, then say: **Let's tell God thank you for these things.**

The children's ministry appreciates the important role that you have volunteered to fill. We are confident that God is going to do amazing things in the lives of our children.

Sincerely,

Children's Ministry Coordinator

StationMaster Card #1

This first week, the children have been taught one reason why people pray: *People pray to show they trust God and depend on Him.* The Bible story comes from Joshua 10.

During your prayer time today, please lead your group in prayer according to the entire imPACT model (praise, ask, confess, and thank). As your children pray, focus their thoughts on today's lesson:

■ *Praise.* **In our Bible story today, we saw how God has control over the elements like the sun and hail. What other natural things does God control?** Let each child praise God for one natural element over which He has control.

■ *Ask.* **Joshua depended on God to help him win the battle. Do you always remember to depend on God? Can you think of a time when you did not? Let's ask God to help us depend on Him more.**

■ *Confess.* **Let's tell God we are sorry for those times we forgot to depend on Him.** You can set an example by asking for forgiveness for not trusting God more with day-to-day things.

■ *Thank.* You have been given the gift of leading a group of children who are precious to God. End your time of prayer by thanking Him for each child in your group.

Remember that no child should be forced to pray, but do encourage and invite each one. After you have said "Amen," keep your group together until the children's ministry coordinator tells everyone about the next activity. During this time, you can quietly talk to the children in your group.

StationMaster Card #2

This week your group discovered a second reason for prayer: *We pray because God is delighted to talk with us.* The Bible story comes from 1 Samuel 16 and Psalm 29.

During prayer time today, please lead your group in prayer according to the entire imPACT model (praise, ask, confess, and thank).

■ *Praise.* **What kinds of things make your parents happy? Do you remember that you can make God happy by talking and listening to Him? Let's praise God that He wants to talk and listen to us.**

■ *Ask.* **David prayed while he watched sheep. When will you talk to God every day?**

Children will ask God to remind them to pray every day at that time.

■ *Confess.* **Think about times this week when you could have talked to God, but you didn't. Tell God you're sorry for not spending that time with Him.**

■ *Thank.* End your time of prayer by thanking God for each child in your group.

Remember that no child should be forced to pray. After you have said "Amen," keep your group together until the children's ministry coordinator tells everyone about the next activity. During this time, you can quietly talk to the children in your group.

StationMaster Card #3

This week your group learned that people pray because *God allows them to be involved in His work.* The Bible story comes from the Book of Esther.

During prayer time today, please lead your group in prayer according to the entire imPACT model (praise, ask, confess, and thank).

■ *Praise.* **How has God used you to make someone happy or learn about Him? God is so great that He gives us a way to be involved in His work.** Have children praise Him for allowing them to be a part of His plan.

■ *Ask.* **Esther was willing to help her people. God wants you to receive the reward of being involved in His work. Let's ask Him who you can help.**

■ *Confess.* **Now is the time we tell God we are sorry for the wrong things we have done. Is there a time when you have disobeyed what you know God wants you to do?** They can ask God for forgiveness.

■ *Thank.* **Let's talk to God about some of the things we are thankful for.** End the time of prayer by thanking God for each child in your group by name.

Remember that no child should be forced to pray. After you have said "Amen," keep your group together until the children's ministry coordinator tells everyone about the next activity. Meanwhile, quietly talk to the children in your group.

StationMaster Card #4

This week your group learned that *people pray because God has told them to pray.* The Bible story from Numbers 22—23 is about Balaam learning to obey God through a talking donkey.

During prayer time today, please lead your group in prayer according to the entire imPACT model (praise, ask, confess, and thank).

- *Praise.* **Think of a time this week when you obeyed your parents or teachers.** Children can praise God that He loves to help them obey.
- *Ask.* **Now think of a time when you knew you should obey, but didn't. Let's pray for a more obedient spirit this week.**
- *Confess.* **Let's tell God how sorry we are for disobeying this week.** Lead children to ask God for forgiveness.
- *Thank.* **Thank God that He's promised to forgive us when we ask, and will help us follow Him. Thank Him too that He loves us as much as always.**

Remember that no child should be forced to pray, but do encourage and invite each one. After you have said "Amen," keep your group together until the children's ministry coordinator tells everyone about the next activity. Meanwhile, talk quietly with the children in your group.

StationMaster Card #5

This week your group discovered that *prayer is a conversation with God;* it is both talking and listening to Him. Bible verses gave five examples of how Jesus talked and listened to the Father.

During prayer time today, please lead your group in prayer according to the entire imPACT model (praise, ask, confess, and thank):

- *Praise.* Have children ask God what He wants to be praised for. **After you quietly listen for God's voice, praise God for whatever things He brings to your mind.**
- *Ask.* Do you need to work more at being a listener or a speaker? Children can ask God to help them either speak or listen better.
- *Confess.* **Think about a time when you didn't talk to God. Now think of another time when you didn't listen to Him. Tell God about those times and that you're sorry.**
- *Thank.* **Thank God that He still speaks to us today. Tell Him thank you for His Word, the Bible.** Close by thanking God for bringing each child to your group.

Remember that no child should be forced to pray. After you say "Amen," keep your group together until the children's ministry coordinator tells everyone about the next activity. Meanwhile, quietly talk to the children.

StationMaster Card #6

This week, the children learned that *we can pray to know God's will*. The Bible story comes from 1 Kings 18:21-39.

During prayer time today, please lead your group in prayer according to the entire imPACT model (praise, ask, confess, and thank). As your children engage in these four activities of prayer, focus their thoughts on today's lesson:

- *Praise.* **God has a perfect will for each of you. Let's praise God because He loves you and me enough to have a wonderful plan for our lives.** Children can praise God for being willing to show them what He wants.
- *Ask.* **Can you know what God wants any time of the day?** (yes) **You only need to talk to Him and He'll help you understand what He wants.** Lead children in asking to show them His will for them and to help them do what He wants them to do.
- *Confess.* **Let's tell God we're sorry when we don't care what He wants. Let's also tell God we're sorry for the times we haven't done what we knew God wanted.**
- *Thank.* **We can thank God that He is the same mighty God today who showed His power in our Bible story today.** End your time of prayer by thanking God that He created each child in your group.

After you have said "Amen," keep your group together until it's time for the next activity. Meanwhile, talk quietly to the children in your group.

StationMaster Card #7

This week the children learned from Luke 7:1-10 that God wants people to *pray with faith*.

During prayer time today, please lead your group in prayer according to the entire imPACT model (praise, ask, confess, and thank). As your children engage in these four activities of prayer, you can further focus their thoughts on today's lesson:

- *Praise.* **Think of one thing God did this week when He wasn't there in His body. Now praise Him for being able to do anything, even when we can't see Him.**
- *Ask.* Ask for prayer requests. **God can do anything if it's in His will and we pray with faith.** Pray with the children for their requests.
- *Confess.* Talk with students about how it can be hard to believe that God can do things without being physically there. **Let's tell God we're sorry for a time this week we didn't think God was there, so we didn't have faith.**
- *Thank.* **Think about something that God has done for you this week. Thank Him for that. Let Him know how you feel about His answer to your prayer.**

Remember that no child should be forced to pray, but do encourage and invite each one. After saying "Amen," keep your group together until the next activity. Meanwhile, quietly talk to your group.

StationMaster Card #8

During prayer time today, please lead your group in prayer according to the imPACT model (praise, ask, confess, and thank). If it is right for your group, you can also focus their thoughts about salvation:

- *Praise.* **God adopts everyone who accepts Him into His family as true sons and daughters. Let's praise God for all He's done to give us a place in heaven.** Don't forget to add your own thanks to God for each child in your group.
- *Ask.* **We all want to go to heaven to be with God.** Help children pray and ask God to be in charge of their lives, and to show them how to live the way He wants them. If they aren't comfortable doing that, then suggest that they can also do this with their parents or even later by themselves.

- *Confess.* **When we disobey God and don't want to do things His way, that's called "sin." Can you think of a time when you didn't want to obey God?** (affirm answers) **The problem with sin is that it separates us from God.** Have children tell God that they're sorry that they sinned.
- *Thank.* **God wants everyone to be with Him. So He sent His Son, Jesus, to die on the cross and take the punishment for our sin. When you told God you were sorry, He forgave you.** Prompt children to tell God thank you for dying on the cross so they can go to heaven.

Remember that no child should be forced to pray, but do encourage and invite each one. After saying "Amen," keep your group together and quietly talk with them.

StationMaster Card #9

This week your group learned that *they should thank God for everything.* The Bible story from Genesis tells how God created the world.

During prayer time today, please lead your group in prayer according to the imPACT model (praise, ask, confess, and thank). As your children engage in these four activities of prayer, you can further focus their thoughts on today's lesson:

- *Praise.* **What things do you really enjoy in creation? Let's praise God for being so creative in making these good things.**
- *Ask.* **Think about all God has done for you. He's provided your clothes, your home, your family, your school, and so much more. Ask God to open your eyes to see all God has**

done for you.
- *Confess.* **God gave His Son, Jesus, to die for our sins. That was a huge sacrifice. Let's tell God we're sorry for what we've done this week that has disappointed God.**
- *Thank.* Go around the group to give each child a chance to thank God for something he or she chooses. In your prayer, thank the Lord for each child in your group.

Don't force any child to pray, but do encourage and invite each one. After you have said "Amen," keep your group together until the next activity. Meanwhile, quietly talk to the children in your group.

StationMaster Card #10

This week your group discovered that *people pray and praise God* for who He is. The Bible story included a list of verses describing some characteristics of God. These attributes help us understand how great God is.

In addition to leading your group according to the entire imPACT model (praise, ask, confess, and thank), you can also do the following for this week:

- *Praise.* **As you pray, tell God what you like most about Him.**
- *Ask.* Give children opportunity to pray for another child's prayer requests.

- *Confess.* **Often we forget to praise God—but He's so deserving of our praise. Right now you can ask His forgiveness for forgetting to tell Him how great He is.**
- *Thank.* Have children thank God for one good thing that happened to them during the last week. And thank God for each child in your group.

Remember that no child should be forced to pray. After you have said "Amen," keep your group together until the next activity. Meanwhile, quietly talk to the children in your group.

StationMaster Card #11

This week children found that they need to *ask God for forgiveness when they do wrong*. The Bible story comes from John 8.

In addition to leading your group according to the entire imPACT model (praise, ask, confess, and thank), you can also help your students focus on the following this week:

- *Praise.* Have students think about a time when someone hurt them and how hard it was to forgive that person. **We hurt God every time we sin, but He always forgives us. Praise God that He is so forgiving.**
- *Ask.* Children can ask God to help them forgive

those who have been mean or done wrong to them.
- *Confess.* **Think about a time when you have hurt someone, on purpose or by accident. Tell God you're sorry and ask Him to forgive you.**
- *Thank.* Have children thank God for forgiving them of all their sins. Then thank God for each child in your group.

Remember that no child should be forced to pray. After you have said "Amen," keep your group together until the next activity. During this time, you can quietly talk to the children in your group.

StationMaster Card #12

This week the children found that an important part of prayer is *listening to God*. Our Bible story was from 1 Samuel 3:1-21.

Today, please lead your group according to the entire imPACT model of prayer (praise, ask, confess, and thank). As your children engage in these four activities of prayer, focus their thoughts on today's lesson.

- *Praise.* Give children a chance to praise God for wanting to talk to them. They might praise Him for being a Friend, Helper, Father, or other attributes.
- *Ask.* **Can you remember a time you haven't listened when you should have? Ask God to help you become a better listener.**
- *Confess.* **Not listening can even get you into trouble. If you haven't listened when you should, and you haven't confessed that to God, now's a good time to do that.**
- *Thank.* **Because Jesus died on the cross, God speaks to us through His Holy Spirit. Thank God for speaking to you through the Bible, other people, and His Holy Spirit.**

Remember that no child should be forced to pray. After you have said "Amen," keep your group together until the next activity. Meanwhile, quietly talk to the children in your group.

StationMaster Card #13   Whole Group Prayer Time

God is everywhere. Unlike us, He hears everything that is said. Though we all talk at once, God can hear each of us individually. As we pray together, you're going to pray on your own, but we'll all do it at the same time.

- *Praise.* **Think about something amazing about God. I'll say, "We praise you, God," and you can say that as a praise to God.**
- *Ask.* Give children a moment to think what they want to ask God for. **When I say, "Please, God," you can ask God for something you need or pray for another person.**
- *Confess.* **Close your eyes and think about this week. If God brings to your mind something you've done wrong, you can confess it to Him. When I say, "Forgive us, God," tell God what you need to confess and ask His forgiveness.**
- *Thank.* **Now we'll thank God. What has God done for you or what prayer has He answered for you? When I say, "Thank You, God," tell Him what you're thankful for.**
- Finally, ask the children to sit still and think about God and listen. Let the room be quiet for about a minute.

If a child chooses not to pray out loud, that is okay. No child should be forced to pray. After you have said "Amen," remind your students that God is everywhere and can hear them even if other people are talking.

On the Fast Track!

Prayer Challenge

Ask your parents or someone in your family to pray with you this week. Together, ask God to help you trust Him more every day. Are there some things for which you need help this week? Tell God about those, too. Tell Him "thank you" that you can depend on Him for everything you need.

Maze

Bible Memory Verse

The LORD is my strength and my shield; my heart trusts in him, and I am helped. My heart leaps for joy and I will give thanks to him in song (Psalm 28:7).

*Note: Early elementary verse in **bold** type.*

Word Search

```
S S A U H S O J
A T Y G N O S E
L O R D K H K L
J P B E I D N T
S C D E N O A T
E E L P G G H A
V D F G S H T B
E I J T R A E H
N K L R W I L L
J O S U N H I M
M F P S N O Y G
P I A T H A I L
Q V E S R V R S
H E L P E D T U
```

(Younger children may have help with this word search.) Find these 18 words hidden in the puzzle.

LORD	JOSHUA
SHIELD	HEART
STOP	TRUSTS
HIM	PRAY
LEAPS	BATTLE
JOY	WILL
GIVE	THANKS
KINGS	SONG
PSALM	SEVEN

Dear Parents and Guardians,

Please check off the items your child completed this week:

❑ Prayer Challenge
❑ Bible verse memorized and recited to an adult
❑ Word Search
❑ Maze

Adult Signature: _____

FAST TRACK! TICKET

On the Fast Track!

Prayer Challenge

Find a place that is quiet. Spend 10 minutes talking and listening to God there. Thank Him for your favorite toys, talk to Him about what you want to be when you grow up, and then talk about anything else that comes to mind. Then listen.

Bible Memory Verse

Blessed is the man . . . [whose] delight is in the law of the LORD, and on his law he meditates day and night (Psalm 1:1-2).

Time to Pray

Write or draw what you can talk to God about at each o'clock (number on the clock).

Hidden Message

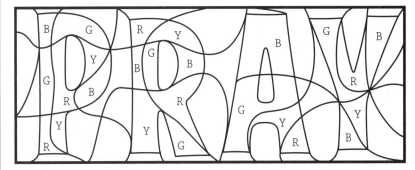

Color all the B's blue, R's red, G's green, and Y's yellow. You will find a hidden message on this page.

Dear Parents and Guardians,

Please check off the items your child completed this week:

☐ Prayer Challenge
☐ Bible verse memorized and recited to an adult
☐ Time to Pray
☐ Hidden Message

Adult Signature: _____

FAST TRACK! TICKET

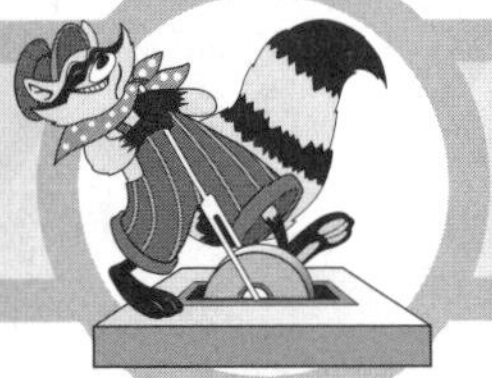

On the Fast Track!

Take-Home Activities #3
God Allows Us to Be Involved in His Work

Prayer Challenge

Write down or draw what you saw God do in your family this week. Especially look for the small things. (Example: Your brothers got along, everyone was healthy, etc.)

Letter Puzzle

In the letter puzzle, you'll find five words (one in each line). These words come from this week's memory verse and Bible lesson. To find the words, you must do the following:

- Circle the following letters: A, D, E, F, H, I, L, M, N, P, R, S, T, Y
- Write the circled letters from each row on the lines below.
- Unscramble the letters to make words from your lesson.

1.	**H**	**V**	**E**	**R**	**W**	**E**	**X**	**S**	**Z**	**B**	**T**	**C**
2.	**G**	**M**	**Q**	**A**	**V**	**W**	**H**	**X**	**A**	**N**	**Z**	**B**
3.	**C**	**G**	**Q**	**V**	**L**	**Y**	**F**	**W**	**M**	**X**	**A**	**I**
4.	**Z**	**B**	**D**	**R**	**C**	**I**	**G**	**S**	**E**	**N**	**F**	**Q**
5.	**R**	**V**	**W**	**X**	**A**	**Z**	**P**	**B**	**C**	**Y**	**G**	**Q**

1. __ __ __ __ __ __
2. __ __ __ __ __
3. __ __ __ __ __ __
4. __ __ __ __ __ __ __
5. __ __ __ __

Bible Memory Verse

For we are God's workmanship, created in Christ Jesus to do good works, which God prepared in advance for us to do (Ephesians 2:10).

Note: *Early elementary verse in* ***bold*** *type.*

Handy Reminder

On a sheet of white paper, trace the hand of each person in your family. Write their names on their hands. Every day this week, look at your family's handprints and pray for each person.

Dear Parents and Guardians,

Please check off the items your child completed this week:

- ❑ Prayer Challenge
- ❑ Bible verse memorized and recited to an adult
- ❑ Handy Reminder
- ❑ Letter Puzzle

Adult Signature: ________________________

FAST TRACK! TICKET

PUZZLE ANSWERS: Esther, Haman, family, friends, pray

On the Fast Track!

Cartoon

Use the boxes below to draw a cartoon about Balaam and his donkey. Color your comic strip with colored pencils or crayons.

Balaam and his donkey travel.	The angel of the Lord stops them.	God uses a donkey to tell Balaam to obey.

Prayer Challenge

God wants us to pray. We pray because God has asked us to. Write the name or draw a person you have trouble getting along with. Tell what makes this person difficult. Pray for this person every day this week. Pray only good things and to be able to get along together.

I have trouble liking _____

because _____

_____.

I prayed for them on
- ❑ Sunday
- ❑ Monday
- ❑ Tuesday
- ❑ Wednesday
- ❑ Thursday
- ❑ Friday
- ❑ Saturday

Puppet Play

Ask your parents for two old white socks. Put one on your hand. Draw two eyes with a marker. Make another puppet for your other hand. Use the cartoon pictures you drew to remind you of the story, and put on a puppet play for your friends. One puppet will be Balaam and the other will be the donkey.

Bible Memory Verse

If you love me, you will obey what I command (John 14:15).

Dear Parents and Guardians,

Please check off the items your child completed this week:

- ❑ Prayer Challenge
- ❑ Bible verse memorized and recited to an adult
- ❑ Cartoon
- ❑ Puppet Play

Adult Signature: _____

FAST TRACK! TICKET

On the Fast Track!

Prayer Challenge

Set aside time to have a new conversation with God. Talk and then listen. Write or draw your conversation.

I asked . . .

God answered . . .

God taught me . . .

Clock Puzzle

Write the words in each numbered blank that matches the numbers that should be on the clock.

_____ _____ _____ _____ _____ _____
6   2   7   11   9   4

_____ _____ _____ _____ _____ _____
10   3   12   1   8   5

Think and Do

Have a conversation with your parents or another adult. Ask them to tell you a story about how God answered their prayers. Write or draw how God answered.

_____ asked . . .

God answered . . .

This is the lesson God was teaching . . .

Bible Memory Verse

I will listen to what God the Lord will say; he promises peace to his people (Psalm 85:8).
Note: Early elementary verse in **bold** *type.*

Dear Parents and Guardians,
Please check off the items your child completed this week:

- ❑ Prayer Challenge
- ❑ Bible verse memorized and recited to an adult
- ❑ Think and Do
- ❑ Clock Puzzle

Adult Signature: _____

FAST TRACK! TICKET

Prayer Challenge

Write or draw one thing from your *Think and Do* list that you want God to help you do. Pray every day this week that God would build this in you.

Think and Do

Look up and read the following verses (you may ask an adult to help you). Beside each verse write a word, or draw a picture, that tells God's will for your life. The first one is done for you.

- Ephesians 5:1-2   Love _____
- Ephesians 5:19   _____
- 1 Thessalonians 4:7   _____
- 1 Thessalonians 5:16   _____
- Ephesians 4:32   _____
- Philippians 2:3-4   _____
- Philippians 2:14   _____

Bible Memory Verse

Your kingdom come, your will be done on earth as it is in heaven (Matthew 6:10).

Puzzle

B	X	T	B	L
W	X	L	O	B
X	R	S	B	L
H	T	I	L	B
B	X	L	L	P

What did the people do after God sent fire and burned Elijah's sacrifice? Color in all the squares with the letters B, X, T, and L. Then write the letters that aren't colored in order on the lines below to find the answer to the question.

___ ___ ___ ___ ___ ___ ___

Dear Parents and Guardians,

Please check off the items your child completed this week:

❑ Prayer Challenge
❑ Bible verse memorized and recited to an adult
❑ Think and Do
❑ Puzzle

Adult Signature: _____

FAST TRACK! TICKET

ANSWER: worship

On the Fast Track!

Prayer Challenge

Walk around your church building with your family. This is called "prayer walking." Pray for your pastors and the people who go to church there. Make sure you ask God if He wants you to pray for anyone else as you walk.

Bible Memory Verse

And without faith it is impossible to please God (Hebrews 11:6).

Think and Do

Make a list or draw pictures of the people who have authority in your life (i.e., parents, police, U.S. president, etc.). Make a list of what God has authority over in your life.

People

_____

_____

_____

_____

_____

God

_____

_____

_____

_____

_____

Decode the Message

1	2	3	4	5	6	7	8	9	10	11	12	13
A	B	C	D	E	F	G	H	I	J	K	L	M

14	15	16	17	18	19	20	21	22	23	24	25	26
N	O	P	Q	R	S	T	U	V	W	X	Y	Z

___ ___ ___ ___ , ___ ___ ___ ___ ___ ___ , ___ ___ ___ ___ ___ ___
12 15 18 4   25 15 21   4 15 14 20   14 5 5 4

___ ___ ___ ___ ___ ___ ___ . ___ ___ ___ ___ ___ ___ ___
20 15   3 15 13 5   19 1 25   20 8 5

___ ___ ___ ___ ___ ___ ___ ___ ___ ___ ___ ___ ___ ___ ___ ___ ___ ___ ___
23 15 18 4   1 14 4   13 25   19 5 18 22 1 14 20

___ ___ ___ ___ ___ ___ ___ ___ ___ ___ ___ ___ .
23 9 12 12   2 5   8 5 1 12 5 4

Dear Parents and Guardians,

Please check off the items your child completed this week:

Adult Signature: _____

❏ Prayer Challenge
❏ Bible verse memorized and recited to an adult
❏ Think and Do
❏ Decode the Message

FAST TRACK! TICKET

Prayer Challenge

Talk and listen to God for 10 minutes this week. Ask Him what He wants you to ask for. Write those things down here, and ask Him for them.

Bible Memory Verse

Call to me and I will answer you and tell you great and unsearchable things you do not know (Jeremiah 33:3).

Think and Do

In the column on the left, write or draw three things God has done for you that you never asked Him to do. In the right column, write or draw three things you want to ask God for (remember that they have to be according to His will).

God Did This for Me	I Ask God for This

Morse Code Puzzle

Study the Morse code below. Then write "Call to me and I will answer you" in Morse code. See if your parents can figure out what you wrote.

A ·–	B –···	C –·–·	D –··	E ·
F ··–·	G ––·	H ····	I ··	J ·–––
K –·–	L ·–··	M ––	N –·	O –––
P ·––·	Q ––·–	R ·–·	S ···	T –
U ··–	V ···–	W ·––	X –··–	Y –·––
Z ––··				

_____

_____

_____

_____

_____

_____

_____

Dear Parents and Guardians,

Please check off the items your child completed this week:

- ☐ Prayer Challenge
- ☐ Bible verse memorized and recited to an adult
- ☐ Think and Do
- ☐ Morse Code Puzzle

Adult Signature: _____

FAST TRACK! TICKET

On the Fast Track!

Prayer Challenge

God wants you to thank Him at all times. Spend some time every day this week thanking God for the things that make you happy. Sometimes things happen that we aren't happy about. What then? Ask God to show you what you can be thankful even when times are hard.

Bible Memory Verse

Be joyful always; pray continually; give thanks in all circumstances, for this is God's will for you in Christ Jesus (1 Thess. 5:16-18). *Note: Early elementary verse in **bold** type.*

Think and Do

God took six days to make all of creation. Read Genesis 1 and 2 (you may have someone help you read it). Put these things in the correct order. Draw a line to connect the event with the day God created it.

Day One	Sun and stars in the sky
Day Two	People
Day Three	Oceans and lakes; plants and trees
Day Four	Fish, water animals, and birds
Day Five	Heavens and earth; light and darkness
Day Six	Waters above and below the sky

Play Dough Recipe

- 2 c. flour
- 1 c. salt
- 4 T. cream of tartar
- 1 pkg. unsweetened dry drink mix for scent and color
- 2 c. warm water
- 2 T. cooking oil

Stir over medium heat until mixture pulls away from sides to form a ball. Store in airtight container. *(for 8 to 10 children)*

Thank You, God

Use the recipe to make play dough with a parent or another helper. As you cook the dough talk about things God has given you that you're thankful for. Then create figures of some of those things with the dough. Show your creations to your family, and tell them why you are thankful for each thing.

Dear Parents and Guardians, *Please check off the items your child completed this week:*

- ☐ Prayer Challenge
- ☐ Bible verse memorized and recited to an adult
- ☐ Think and Do
- ☐ Thank You, God

Adult Signature: _____

FAST TRACK! TICKET

On the Fast Track!

Think and Do

It takes practice to be a good listener. One day this week, tell your parents that you're going to do your best to listen when they speak to you. How did you do? Ask your parents to fill out this chart at the end of the day.

Listening Chart

	Not at all				*Perfectly*
1. _____ listened when I asked him/her to do chores.	1	2	3	4	5
2. _____ paid attention to directions.	1	2	3	4	5
3. _____ listened to everything I said today.	1	2	3	4	5
4. How can I get better at listening? _____					

Read what your parent wrote about your listening habits. On the back, write or draw two ideas about how you can improve your listening skills with God's help.

Prayer Challenge

Every day this week, spend one minute talking to God and five minutes listening. Here are some ways to hear God:

- ■ *In your heart, you will have peace.*
- ■ *Through other people who love God.*
- ■ *By reading the Bible. Ask an adult to help read Psalm 1.*
- ■ *When things happen around you, you can see God working.*

On the back, write down or draw what God said to you this week.

Listen–Talk–Listen

When we pray, we talk and listen to God. This tic-tac-toe game will help you think about talking and listening. Play with a friend. Try to get three "Listens" in a row.

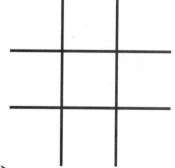

Bible Memory Verse

Be still and know that I am God; I will be exalted among the nations, I will be exalted in the earth (Psalm 46:10). ***Note:*** *Early elementary verse in* **bold** *type.*

Dear Parents and Guardians,

Please check off the items your child completed this week:

- ❑ Prayer Challenge
- ❑ Bible verse memorized and recited to an adult
- ❑ Think and Do
- ❑ Listen–Talk–Listen

Adult Signature: _____

FAST TRACK! TICKET

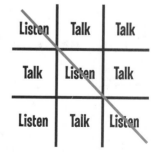

Listen	Talk	Talk
Talk	Listen	Talk
Listen	Talk	Listen

On the Fast Track!

Prayer Challenge— Hide 'n' Seek Prayer

Before playing this game, you need to collect five prayer needs or praises from other people. Besides your family, you can ask a friend, a neighbor, a teacher or coach, a relative, a teammate, or others what you can pray about for them. Play the game with a brother, sister, or friend by hiding somewhere in your house or outside. When your friend finds you, first thank God that He knew where you were all along. Then pray for one of the five needs. Hide in a different place every day, and pray for a different need.

Bible Memory Verse

O LORD, you have searched me and you know me. You know when I sit and when I rise; you perceive my thoughts from afar (Psalm 139:1-2). *Note: Early Elementary verse in* **bold** *type.*

Sun 'n' Moon Maze

Use this space to draw a maze for younger children. Make lines that start at the sun and end at the moon to show that God will hear us day and night.

Everywhere Collage

You can talk to God anytime and anyplace because He is *always with you*. Make a collage of all the times and places God is with you. Cut pictures out of magazines and glue them to a big piece of paper. When you're finished, show your collage to your family and tell them about each picture.

Dear Parents and Guardians,
Please check off the items your child completed this week:

- ❏ Prayer Challenge
- ❏ Bible verse memorized and recited to an adult
- ❏ Everywhere Collage
- ❏ Sun 'n' Moon Maze

Adult Signature: _____

FAST TRACK! TICKET

On the Fast Track!

Prayer Challenge

Turn on a praise song (on the radio or a CD) and sing, or sing a praise song from your church once a day. Think about how awesome God is.

Bible Memory Verse

Let everything that has breath praise the LORD. Praise the LORD (Psalm 150:6).

Matching

Look up the verses on the left (you may have someone help you). Then draw a line matching the verse to the description of God on the right.

1 John 4:14	All-knowing
Psalm 111:4	King of kings
1 John 4:16	Ever-Present
Psalm 19:14	Mighty God
Psalm 91:2	Fortress
Revelation 11:17	Compassionate
1 Timothy 6:15	Lamb of God
Isaiah 9:6	Love
Hebrews 10:30	Rock and Redeemer
Genesis 1:1	Holy
Psalm 139:1	God Almighty
Psalm 139:7-8	Judge
Psalm 99:9	Savior
John 1:29	Creator

Plan a Pennant

Choose one Bible verse in the "Matching" puzzle at the left to make your own praise pennant. Cut a sheet of paper into a triangle. On one side of the paper, write down the Bible verse reference. On the other side, draw and color a picture that reminds you of that characteristic of God. Glue a stick to one side of the paper to make a flag. Put it somewhere in your room as a reminder.

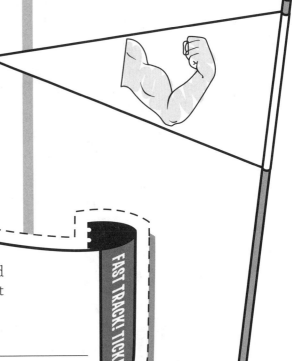

Dear Parents and Guardians,

Please check off the items your child completed this week:

- ❏ Prayer Challenge
- ❏ Bible verse memorized and recited to an adult
- ❏ Matching
- ❏ Plan a Pennant

Adult Signature: _____

FAST TRACK! TICKET

On the Fast Track!

Prayer Challenge

Ask God this week to help you forgive others who have hurt you or made you angry. Then think about times when you've disobeyed God. Tell Him you're sorry. Thank Him that He forgives you when you ask.

Bible Memory Verse

For if you forgive men when they sin against you, your heavenly Father will also forgive you (Matthew 6:14).

Think and Do

Did someone hurt you or make you angry last week? _____

What happened? _____

_____

_____

Did you forgive him or her? _____

Who did you hurt last week? _____

_____

Did you ask for forgiveness? _____

How do you think you disappointed God last week? _____

_____

_____

Did you ask for forgiveness? _____

Kindness Counts

Think about the person who hurt you last week. Did you forgive him or her? Now go out of your way to do one nice thing for that person this week. Be sure to tell a parent or another adult what you did.

Dear Parents and Guardians,

Please check off the items your child completed this week:

- ❏ Prayer Challenge
- ❏ Bible verse memorized and recited to an adult
- ❏ Think and Do
- ❏ Kindness Counts

Adult Signature: _____

FAST TRACK! TICKET